**W9-AMX-775**

# The Stories of Raymond Carver

# The Stories
# of Raymond Carver
## A CRITICAL STUDY
Kirk Nesset

Ohio University Press

*Athens*

Ohio University Press, Athens, Ohio 45701
© 1995 by Kirk Nesset
Printed in the United States of America
All rights reserved
99  98  97  96  95    5  4  3  2  1
Ohio University Press books are printed on acid-free paper ∞

Library of Congress Cataloging-in-Publication Data
Nesset, Kirk.
    The stories of Raymond Carver : a critical study / Kirk Nesset.
        p.    cm.
    Includes bibliographical references (p.     ) and index.
    ISBN 0-8214-1099-7 (cloth). — ISBN 0-8214-1100-4 (paperback)
    1. Carver, Raymond—Criticism and interpretation.
2. Postmodernism (Literature)—United States.    3. Realism in
literature.   4. Short story.   I. Title.
PS3553.A7894Z78    1994
813'.54—dc20                                        94-30322
                                                        CIP

For V. V.

# Contents

# Acknowledgements

ABOVE ALL I OWE THANKS here to William Stull, Carver's bibliographer and foremost champion, not only for the many fine books and essays he has published by and about Carver but also for his willingness to correspond on these matters — for the many letters and phone calls we exchanged, for his generosity and unwavering patience, and for that fine Vietnamese meal back in Hartford. I am also grateful to Tess Gallagher, whose blessing means very much to me, and whose comments were invaluable to this project (chapter 4 in particular). Thanks are due, too, to Steven Allaback, for his good judgment and honesty, and for the use of his refuge one summer, his sunny house by the sea. I am thankful as well to Steven Jensen for his sharp editorial eye, and to Pam Hengst at Whittier College, for all her secretarial help. Finally, I am indebted to the editors of *American Literature*, *Essays in Literature*, and *Profils Americains*, both for publishing chapters of this manuscript (or parts of chapters, some in slightly different form) and for their permission to reprint that material here.

K. N.

# Introduction

RAYMOND CARVER WAS BORN IN 1938 in Clatskanie, Oregon, a small sawmill town near the Columbia River. After graduating from high school he worked at the mill with his father (a hard drinking laborer who had migrated west from Arkansas), married shortly after his nineteenth birthday, and had two children within the first eighteen months of his marriage. Carver moved to California in 1958 and enrolled at Chico State College, where, pressed by financial worries, he worked "crap jobs," as he called them, to support his family. Two years later he transferred to Humboldt State College to finish his degree, during which time he began publishing his first poems and stories in little magazines. By the early seventies his literary reputation had grown to the extent that he began accepting visiting appointments at universities, although as a result of his drinking — which worsened steadily in the seventies, and nearly killed him before he gave it up in 1977 — his early teaching career was anything but ideal.

The nature of Carver's success — his meteoric rise to international acclaim, his widespread appeal, his continuing influence on American letters — seems all the more extraordinary in light of such inauspicious beginnings. Between 1976 and 1988 he published ten books of poetry and prose, as well as numerous chapbooks and limited editions. An eleventh book, another collection of poems, appeared in 1989, the year after he died. He was the recipient of many awards, including a Guggenheim Fellowship, Poetry magazine's Levinson Prize, a National Book Circle Critics Award, the prestigious Mildred and Harold Strauss Living Award, nominations for the Pulitzer Prize, and an honorary Doctorate of Letters from

Hartford University. Among other things, Carver has been dubbed the rejuvenator of the dying American short story, the godfather of literary "minimalism," and in light of recent trends in American writing, the most imitated American writer since Hemingway.

Despite the happy circumstances of the final decade of Carver's life, however — despite literary recognition, despite his victory over alcohol, and, after a trying divorce, his fortuitous linking with and marriage to writer Tess Gallagher — his work continued to reflect the difficult circumstances of his former life. From the earliest story to the last, Carver's characters are unhappily estranged, out of work, disillusioned by meaningless jobs and meaningless marriages; they suffer in various degrees from alcoholism as well as bad luck and bad timing, battered by a world which typically leaves them inert and speechless in the wake of longings and fears they cannot begin to identify. The "trademark Carver tale," one critic writes, "is a kind of mundane ghost story in which . . . people are haunted by the presence of some lost, almost forgotten, not-really-expected possibility."[1] Alienated from ideals and aspirations they only dimly comprehend, and ultimately from themselves, Carver's figures play out, in the words of another critic, "the terrifying implications of Normal Life." Dreading the approach of the bill collector, knocked down by marital infidelity or the torments of delirium tremens, they live out "normal nightmares" from which they rarely awake.[2] And yet while such scenarios reflect to an extent the darkest periods of Carver's early married life, they also attest to his triumph, to that miraculous recovery of sorts, and to Carver's uncanny capacity for transforming life into art, for erecting a monument to pain even as he learned to transcend it.

Unique as the stories are in subject and manner, one need not look far to see how securely Carver's fiction is rooted in a recognizable literary tradition. With elliptical spareness and precision, alive with repetition though flattened by his characteristic deadpan tone, Carver's prose hearkens back obviously to Hemingway (with an important distinction concerning voice: as Jay McInerney observes, Carver has dispensed with the "romantic egoism" which makes the "Hemingway idiom such an awkward model for other writers in the late 20th century").[3] Carver's style — starkly terse, vibrating with unspoken energies of indecision, dread and half-hearted expectation, modulating in mood from darkly humorous to

grim to positively eerie — also draws notably from Kafka, whose uncanny moods are evoked in the coupling of hyper-rational prose with sur-
real, irrational scenarios and events. Carver's subjects, in similar fashion,
place him squarely in a tradition of American prose writing, fixing him at
the end of a trajectory extending from Sherwood Anderson to John
O'Hara to John Cheever, and mirroring another trajectory, a Russian one,
extending from Turgenev to Chekov, writers in whom Carver was in-
tensely interested. Carver's subjects, in other words, are aligned with
those of authors who have for decades given voice to the woes and disen-
chantments of modern (industrial, urban, suburban) life. Cheever,
Carver's immediate predecessor — whom Carver befriended in Iowa
(employed briefly as teachers, the two enjoyed days-long drinking binges
together) — made a living recapitulating this obsession, giving voice to
the enchantment of American disenchantment. Cheever perhaps summed
it up best in "The Death of Justina":

There are some Americans who, although their fathers emigrated from the Old
World three centuries ago, never seem to have quite completed the voyage and I am
one of these. I stand, figuratively, with one wet foot on Plymouth Rock, looking
with some delicacy, not into a formidable and challenging wilderness but onto a
half-finished civilization embracing glass towers, oil derricks, suburban continents,
and abandoned movie houses and wondering why, in this most prosperous, equi-
table, and accomplished world — where even the cleaning women practice the
Chopin preludes in their spare time — everyone should seem to be disappointed.[4]

Hovering near the end of this continuum of dashed hopes and disillusionment, Carver's characters are noticeably more disappointed than
Cheever's. Given the severity of their predicaments and their limited powers of apprehension, they tend to lack both the capacity and the impetus
necessary for the task of "wondering why." Springing in turn from
Anderson's "grotesques" and Cheever's unhappy suburbanites, Carver's
figures take American disappointment to its barest extreme, haunted as
they are by unfulfillable, intangible longings, paralyzed, lost, pushed well
beyond the verge of articulate dismay. Unlike Cheever's characters,
Carver's cannot speak their pain. They translate it instead into obsessive
behavior, into desperate and abusive patterns, into drinking, smoking,
and eating, into adultery, into voyeurism and, on occasion, violence —

behavior linked, as Paul Skenazy observes, "to a sense of failure and a recognition of the gap between American possibilities and their own hard lot."[5] Recording the obsessions and the bafflements of a class of people he knows only all too well, Carver probes, as Irving Howe notes, "the waste and destructiveness that prevail beneath the affluence of American life."[6]

Due perhaps to the gravity of what all of this implies — to the way it reflects, as Carver hesitatingly put it once, the "dark side of Reagan's America" — Carver and his peers and followers have come under fire from conservative critics, those unable or unwilling, caught up in the tide of the eighties, to see beyond the "happy face" taped on the nation in what now seems a temporary, if lopsided, economic prosperity.[7] Along with Frederick Barthelme, Ann Beattie, Richard Ford, Amy Hempel, Bobbie Ann Mason, Mary Robison, Tobias Wolff and others, Carver has been classified and dismissed by some as a "minimalist" — an unfortunate label, considering its sloppy connection to the disciplines from which it was borrowed, and considering the fact that the practitioners of literary "minimalism" boast in general far more differences than similarities in terms of individual craft. Still, the various complaints about the new prose — paucity of narrative, the so-called deterministic handling of characters, and the political implications of some of the stories — are by far outweighed by favorable appraisals, and by the incredible (and to some, perhaps, alarming) degree of influence and success the new fiction has enjoyed in the marketplace.

One of the most useful commentaries to date is Kim Herzinger's "On the New Fiction," appearing in an edition of *The Mississippi Review* devoted entirely to American "minimalists." Herzinger characterizes "new fiction" by its "equanimity of surface, 'ordinary' subjects, recalcitrant narrators and deadpan narratives, slightness of story, and characters who don't think out loud." He also draws attention to the new fiction's "distaste for irony" — a crucial observation — as well as its refusal, in defiance of more traditional brands of realism, to define character through location and setting.[8] "Minimalist" work varies greatly, of course, ranging from Carver's flinty precisionism to Ford's brooding telling-it-like-it-is to Mason's terse down-home prose (replete with product names and television jingles), but such are the qualities characterizing the new fiction in general. Despite its novelty, however, despite its typical hardness in manner and subject, its non-geographicality and anti-ironic demeanor, the fiction constitutes above all a striking resurgence of the realist mode. Along with the prose of his peers, Carver's embodies a realism so rarefied and distilled that critics in their boundless affection for neologisms have dubbed it variously "hyperrealism," "superrealism" and "photorealism." If Carver's work is realism indeed — as Mr. Spock might observe, puzzling over alien life forms — it is not realism as we have formerly known it.

New realism — the new fiction, minimalism — has not emerged at this point in time, at this stage of literary history, without visible cause. Among other things it is a formal reaction to the literary forms of the immediate past, to the baroque, long-winded projects of postmodernists with their labyrinthine plots, or with no plots at all. "Like most excessive states," Skenazy writes, "minimalism [is a] reaction, a kind of austerity program in a time of rhetorical inflation. It is a way of cleaning house, making do with less, the literary equivalent of functionalist architecture."[9] As John Barth puts it, "the more or less minimalist authors of the New American Short Story are re-enacting a cyclical correction in the history . . . of literature and of art in general."[10] By returning to traditional narrative structure — by shunning the example of their immediate postmodern forbears, embracing realism in a way that hones it down as never before, making it distinctly new, distinctly their own — Carver and his fellows have in a very real way cut short the progress of postmodernism's inward spiral, moving radically away from that obsessively self-reflexive, highly ironic, fabulistic, narrative-subverting tendency dominating the work of their predecessors.[11] The minimality of the minimalists stands in direct proportion to the excesses of Barth and Barthelme and Pynchon and Coover and Gaddis and Gass, veering away from the immediate past by returning to a more distant one.[12]

Still, it would be naive to imagine any group of artists to be capable of reacting seriously against their forbears without assimilating them in the process, without appropriating those forbears in some way even as they modify them, or correcting an aesthetic vision they deem past its prime. Thus even as Carver and others have cut away excesses of the past, the concerns of postmodernism are reinscribed in their writings, which makes the new realism a kind of post-postmodern modernism. (The new realism, curiously enough, is to postmodern fiction what modernism was to the Victorian age of prose, with a subtle twist: where modernism subverted traditional, realistic, Victorian narrative structure and characterization by means of fragmentation and radical subjectivity, the new realism subverts the conventions of postmodernist prose by insisting on reality — by bringing traditional narrative back into circulation and reconstituting it, imprinting it with a stamp more grimly "real" than the realism of the past.) [13] In this sense, postmodernism's obsession with the limits of language finds literal, concrete embodiment in the pages of the new realists, in their inarticulate characters and circular, ineffective conversations, and in the lean distribution of descriptive detail overall. Likewise, the trademark postmodern paranoia, that sense of suspicion if not helplessness in the face of the "system" — of the bewilderingly complicated, sinister, self-governing processes of politics and culture and history immortalized, say, by the flustered characters and self-entangling plots of Gaddis and Pynchon — is now manifested in the individual bewilderments of new-realist characters, in the weighty silences of Beattie and Carver and the resigned compromises of Wolff and Ford, silences and compromises illustrating not so much the incomprehensibility and intricacy of the "system" as the extent to which people are bent by it, and how resilient, how durable, they can become in time.

Most important, certainly — explain as we may, stepping tentatively into this age of new-realist postmodern-modernism, into the post-postmodern age — the new fiction has caught on. Its appeal and influence is wide. After nearly two decades of dormancy, the short story is alive and well again in North America — and Raymond Carver, foremost among a handful of writers, has been credited for its revival. Not surprisingly, what began as a new strain of short story ended up leaching out in all directions, prompting a number of American novelists, particularly young ones. In the novels of Susan Minot, David Leavitt, and Brett Easton Ellis, for instance, the ring of Carver is unmistakable. (Jay McInerney, one of the more distinguished novelists of recent years, was one of Carver's pupils, and has written at length about his debt to his former teacher and about what we owe Carver as a pioneer writer.) [14] "The current profusion in the writing and publishing of short stories," Carver wrote in 1987,

"is . . . the most eventful literary phenomenon of our time. It has pro-
vided the tired blood of mainstream American letters with something
new to think about and even — any day now, I suspect — something to
take off from . . . the fact is the resurgence of interest in the short story
has done nothing less than revitalize the national literature." [15]

In the chapters that follow, I discuss individually each of Carver's major press collections of stories: *Will You Please Be Quiet, Please, What We Talk
About When We Talk About Love, Cathedral,* and the "new" stories in *Where
I'm Calling From* (which reprints selected stories, along with seven uncollected works). Except in glancing discussions, I have chosen to overlook
Carver's second volume of stories, *Furious Seasons;* small press production
that it was, it is now largely unavailable to readers, and is comprised of
early, more or less formative stories, that are unrepresentative of Carver's
main body of work. Due to space considerations, I also neglect Carver's
substantial corpus of poetry, which amounts to five volumes, although I
do touch upon a number of poems as illuminating complements to the
stories. [16]

This project is a preliminary exploration and assessment of Carver's
fiction, as any first full-scale critical investigation of an author should be.
By scrutinizing individual stories meticulously and reverberating out,
seeking correspondences and convergences, identifying patterns, tying
together Carver's achievement as a unifiable corpus, I hope to help pave
the way for Carver studies of the future, as well as enhance understanding
and appreciation for those stories whose opaqueness have already raised
thorny interpretive questions in various quarters. Carver's fiction, in a
characteristically modernist way, *invites* close reading (although the power
of the stories is self-evident without it); my critical methods throughout
are accordingly formalist, New Critical in a postmodern-modernist, if
old-fashioned, way. Wary nevertheless of practicing formalism for formalism's sake, I often widen my focus to speculate on the ways Carver's
figures dramatize and indirectly comment upon the problems besetting
American culture, particularly lower middle-class culture, today. I do not
come to these texts armed with a "methodology" (besides a handful of
interpretive tools furnished us long ago by the New Critics) or anything
resembling one, unless in the form of phantom methodologies emerging
in the subtextual shadows of this study, acquired haphazardly and uncon-

sciously in my readings of recent literary theory, feminist and Marxist critiques chief among them. At the heart of my interpretive enterprise, unfashionable as it may sound, is a moral imperative, to a large degree generated by what I have come to recognize as a moral center radiating at the core of Carver's aesthetic. It is no secret that Carver was a pupil of John Gardner, author of *On Moral Fiction* and certainly one of the most outspoken critics of his time; and while Carver has expressed his reservations about aspects of his mentor's controversial book, and while his art bears little overt resemblance to his teacher's, Carver has in many ways betrayed Gardner's influences, his deep moral fibres, both in interviews and in the embedded implications of the stories. Explaining his "problems with some of the postmodernist writers of the Sixties," Carver says that he is above all "interested in stories and poems that have some bearing on how we live and how we conduct ourselves and how we work out the consequences of our actions." [17] One of Gardner's remarks about art in general, in fact, might be taken as a credo for both Carver's and Gardner's work: "Art builds temporary walls against life's leveling force," Gardner writes; "Art rediscovers, generation by generation, what is necessary to humanness." [18]

Taking my cue from Carver, who in turn takes his from Gardner and others, I am as interested in what the stories suggest about the problems of American experience as I am in how they present those problems. The full force of the humanitarian impulses in Carver's fiction comes to a head in *Cathedral* — most notably in the title story, a story about a blind man who teaches a man blinded by prejudice lessons in common humanity, helping him imagine the "temporary walls" of a gothic church. But such impulses operate in Carver's work from the beginning, as in "Fat," an early story about an unhappy waitress who finds humanity in the form of an obese man, humanity at once obscenely visible and, in her eyes, mysteriously compelling. As for Gardner, the word "human" is a touchstone for Carver. It not only comes up repeatedly in his conversations but also, in substantial if tacit ways, resonates in every aspect of his work, from the darkest story to the most joyful poem. The best short stories of our time, as Carver says, keep us in touch with what is "recognizably human" about ourselves and others, transforming us in ways we cannot always comprehend. [19]

# Chapter One

"THIS WORD LOVE": SEXUAL POLITICS AND SILENCE IN *Will You Please Be Quiet, Please?*

*Omnia vincit Amor: et nos cedamus Amori.*

One of the more striking things about Carver's first volume of stories is that as a collection it is hardly uniform in subject or voice. Instead, it embodies what William Stull calls Carver's "formative years," providing, as another critic writes, an exploration of "a common plight rather than a common subject."[1] In *Will You Please Be Quiet, Please?* Carver ranges from the Kafkaesque expressionism of "The Father" to the anecdotal simplicity of "Nobody Said Anything" to the heavier, mildly Faulknerian prose of "Sixty Acres" (in keeping with the style of earlier stories published later in *Furious Seasons*), and he ranges with similar freedom from subject to subject. Despite such diversity, a number of constants arise in the volume, elements marking out the stylistic and the thematic path Carver will follow in the course of his literary career. Most prevalent among these constants is the issue of love — or, more precisely, the issue of love and its absence, and the bearing of love's absence on marriage and individual identity. "His Jamesian donnee was marriage," Stull writes, referring to the early work, and "in particular," he adds, citing Carver, " 'a certain terrible kind of domesticity' that he termed 'dis-ease.' "[2] Even this early, love and its maladies are already an "obsession" for Carver (he hated the word "theme"). With the appearance of his next volume, *What We Talk About When We Talk About Love*, love takes full predominance, figuring as the organizational device, as its title attests; one reviewer describes the work as "a set of variations on the themes of marriage, infidelity and the disquieting tricks of human affection" — an assessment applicable to Carver's first book of fiction as well.[3]

Many of these "disquieting tricks" Carver addresses in his poems, which tend to deal more straightforwardly with his obsessions than do the stories. In 1976 — the year *Will You Please* went to press — Carver brought out a chapbook of poems called *At Night the Salmon Move*, a slim, limited-edition book concluding with a poem called "This Word Love":

> I will not go when she calls
> even if she says I love you,
> especially that,
> even though she swears
> and promises nothing
> but love love.

> The light in this room
> covers every
> thing equally;
> my arm throws no shadow even,
> it too is consumed with light.

> But this word love —
> this word grows dark, grows
> heavy and shakes itself
> and begins to eat
> through this paper.
> Listen.[4]

In Carver's early stories, as in this poem, love is a darkly unknowable and irreversible force, a sickness of sorts that not only complicates but dominates lives. Characters are alternately bewildered, enraged, diminished, suffocated, isolated, and entrapped by love, though unlike the speaker of the poem, who acknowledges the power love exerts over his life, they rarely recognize their circumstances as such. As the word "grows dark" in their lives — as love begins to eat through them, and they find themselves either betraying or betrayed, trapped in a kind of sexuality they cannot understand — they become partakers of sexual politics that not only bring on love's sicknesses but, like bad medicine, worsen the malady. For Carver's lovers, the politics of sex ultimately reflect a kind of larger politics, more tenuous and more ominous still: the politics of fortune and fate which, forever unseen and unheard, dictate the bleak circumstances of their lives, provoking the bafflement and dismay that is for them a daily fact of existence. Evoked by the politics of Carver's uniquely hardscrabble domesticity, the marriages of Will You Please are scaled-down models representing larger, more terrifying politics, or antipolitics — models reflecting, in human form, the arbitrariness and caprice and chaos of the world in which those marriages are rooted.

Just as strikingly, the individual failures of characters (their ailing and broken marriages in particular) are recapitulated in the individual failures of their tongues. Like the speaker of "This Word Love," they are struck dumb by love's buffetings; they wait, they "Listen," and there, usually, Carver leaves them, disconcerted, expectant, lingering passively at the edge of despair. Thus another constant in Will You Please Be Quiet, Please?, as its title suggests, is the issue of language and its limitations (the second volume also picks up this issue, with its emphasis on "talk"). As many critics have observed, this issue is spelled out in the stories as inarticulateness in the brooding silences of characters, a phenomenon mirrored and enhanced by the spareness of what has been aptly dubbed Carver's "unforgiving prose."[5] Still, despite such limitations — despite what many characters sense to be a built-in system of failure — Carver's is not a despairing world. "Raymond Carver's America is helpless," Michael Wood writes, "clouded by pain and the loss of dreams, but it is not as fragile as it looks. It is a place of survivors and a place of stories."[6] The survivors who people these stories, as Carver says in an interview, "do the best they can" given the nature of their circumstances.[7] They talk, however unsuccessfully; they have sex, or avoid it. They employ both their bodies and tongues in efforts to find themselves again, struggling to reassemble the bits and pieces of their tattered identities, and they continue struggling, even as their bodies get them into trouble and their tongues, taking them forever in circles, fall silent.

Perhaps the most frequently commented-upon of Carver's stories — after "Cathedral" and "A Small, Good Thing" — is "Neighbors," a tale of marriage in the process of diminishing. As with so many of Carver's fictive marriages, the story deals less with love or passion than with its conspicuous absence, and with the symptoms of love's withdrawal. It is the tale of Bill and Arlene Miller, a "happy couple" who, now that the original intensity of their marriage has dwindled, experience sexual titillation in the home of their neighbors, which they have agreed to look after (a story that Joyce Carol Oates borrows for "Harrow Street at Linden," a more graphic representation of an identical titillation and its effects). As in "The Idea," a story concerned specifically with voyeurism, "Neighbors" presents a pair of figures who, as Arthur Saltzman notes of Carver's early characters in general, are "obsessed with vicariousness."[8] Affected by overintimacy and the fading vitality of their marriage, they look outward, imagining themselves as others, seeking alternate, more attractive selves.

"[N]ow and then," we learn early in the story, the Millers "felt they alone among their circle had been passed by somehow."[9] Planting themselves amidst the articles and residual energies of their vacationing friends, they experience vicariously a "fuller and brighter life." With its plants and perhaps lurid photographs, with strangely exotic clothes available for the trying on — the "Hawaiian" shirts and "Bermudas" and brassieres and panties — the neighbors' apartment is for the Millers, as Stull writes, a "psychosexual rumpus room" whose influence is not altogether bad.[10] "As the time they spend in the neighbors' apartment lengthens," Ann Beattie observes of the Millers, "their energy begins to bond them together, revitalizing their own marriage."[11] Suddenly reinfused with new life, vicariousness fanning the flames of erotic desire, they become conspirators, lovers attempting jointly to know the sexual selves of a couple whose existence seems more attractive than their own. But the Millers' psychosexual games are not without their negative implications. As David Boxer and Cassandra Phillips have noted, Carver's characters are often not simply voyeurs but "voyeurs . . . of their own experience," seekers in perilous games of peek-a-boo which, if carried far enough, yield "sudden, astonishing glimpses behind the curtain which separates their empty lives from chaos."[12] Carver is expert at "describing various types of emotional parasitism," as one critic says referring to "Neighbors," seeing in the story that form of "dis-ease" which, as the story's ending suggests, results in psychic losses that far outrun erotic gains.[13] Leaving the neighbor's apartment after his first visit, Bill pauses, having "the feeling he had left something" inside. What both Bill and his wife leave behind are, in fact, themselves: shreds of the identities they have been trying self-destructively to nourish in their daily visitations across the hall — shreds that have grown, visit by visit, increasingly malnourished. Finally locked out of their new paradise, and too jaded in the end to appreciate the old quiet ways of the past, they are in "limbo" (as Boxer and Phillips put it), and thus, "dissociated from both lives, the Millers only have each other."[14]

Late twentieth-century versions of Dante's Paolo and Francesca, Bill and Arlene wait in the hall, poised between lives. "They stayed there," the story's concluding sentences read; "They held each other. They leaned into the door as if against a wind, and braced themselves." Like Dante's lovers, they are intimate even in despair, but unlike their precursors, they are battered not by the winds of passion, by love out of control. Instead, Carver's lovers brace themselves against the consequences of inauthentic passion, a false kind of love which, requiring its stimulus from outside influence, feeds on the attractive possibilities of other worlds and other lives at the cost of self. In "The Idea," similarly, where "the voyeur motif is carried to an extreme," an older couple peer out their window, making a nightly ritual of watching the man next door, who stands outside his own window watching his wife undress.[15] Fully corrupted by inauthenticity, their sexual energies as dead as their verbal interchanges in general (and redirected now into eating, the only act — besides voyeurism — in which they partake with any zeal), this couple is the aging, decaying version of Bill and Arlene, a preview of the Millers' ghost-life to come. Following the path of Vern and his wife in "The Idea," the Millers toy with borrowed versions of love, conspiring to bankrupt themselves, both sexually and spiritually.

It is no coincidence, then, that as they embrace in the frantic final moments of the story they both refer to "God." As Arlene realizes they are locked out of their new world — which represents for them not just paradise but also, ironically, Eden, the lost innocence of their early married life — she exclaims, "My God . . . I left the key inside." Bill, trying to reassure her, responds in kind: "For God's sake," he says, "don't worry."

They have had not a single vital verbal interchange in the story, remarkably, until now, when, with an explosive suddenness of vitality, they cling to one another and indirectly call on God, invoking that abstract authority who is for them, in some way or another, the keeper of the larger keys. But the Millers' burst of verbal exuberance and physical intimacy is simultaneously a bang and a whimper. Their unconscious invocations of abstract authority (they are no churchgoers, certainly) testify to the degree of their powerlessness in the face of determined circumstance. Not only are they shut out, cut off from the possibilities of a "fuller and brighter life" in the future; they are also deprived of their past. Growing ever more desensitized, they shall know now only the imprisoning limbo of the present, that numbing atemporal world in which God is just one of many authorities authorizing hard knocks. Enacting the earlier fall of Vern and his wife — who, more sheltered by age and custom, are blown from the outside, their house buffeted by winds — Bill and Arlene "brace themselves" against the limbic winds of mediocrity and, when the words run out, reach out and hold on, comforting themselves the best way they can, while they can.

Love, as Oscar Wilde once so glibly put it, is a malady most often curable by marriage. In "Fat," as in many other stories, Carver explores this unfortunate and sometimes brutal reality, this time taking on the persona of a woman in a story of love gone sour, love that, though still as fresh as week-old milk in "Neighbors," was on the point of turning. It is a frametale in which a waitress, disillusioned with her job and her marriage, explains to a friend her mysterious attraction to an obese customer she has lately served. "I know now I was after something," she tells Rita, her friend, trying to get a handle on her fascination for the man. "But I don't know what." As the story unfolds we understand gradually that the waitress is being suffocated by her husband Rudy, with whom she both lives and works, and that in some curious way the fat man represents to her everything Rudy lacks. Polite, articulate and "well-dressed," the fat man is the token of a kind of opulence and gracious affability which makes the waitress's own dull life seem lean and shabby by comparison.[16]

More than a simple and grossly exaggerated symbol of another life, and more also than a means for retaliation on the part of the narrator (it is suggested, obliquely, that a flirtation is going on between Rudy and another waitress), the fat man is a being with whom, on a deeper, personal level, the narrator strongly identifies. His verbal tick, the sustained use of the royal "we," not only evokes regalness, that tired nobility which so moves the waitress; it evokes even more immediately a kind of complicity, a victimization common to fat man and waitress both. At the one point in their conversings in which they deviate from business — from the business of ordering and eating — the fat man says about the compulsive nature of his gorging, "If we had our choice, no. But there is no choice." Just as he is at the mercy of his appetite, and whatever lies behind that ("he is fat," the waitress tells her husband, "but that is not the whole story"), she too is at the mercy of her world, oppressed by a husband and work environment insensitive to her needs.

Like Nan in "The Student's Wife," the waitress shares her bed with a man with whom she has little in common, with a man who is, like the "businessmen" she daily serves at work, "very demanding." Feeling more distant from her husband than ever after her meeting with the fat man (and after Rudy, in his one talkative moment in the story, says exactly the wrong thing, describing the "fat guys" of his childhood), she "can't think of anything to say" and, undressing, gets into bed, moving "clear over to the edge." As she expects, however, "Rudy begins." Rudy's insistence furnishes physical testimony to what she has heard earlier, at the table of the fat man — there is "no choice" in such matters. Thus she allows Rudy to carry on, admitting nevertheless, as she tells Rita, that "it is against [her] will." Such compliance is, at the extreme — as another of Carver's reluctantly compliant females makes evident — a kind of violence like unto death: witness Claire's sexual acquiescence in "So Much Water So Close to Home," in which she identifies herself, water roaring in her ears, with a raped and murdered woman found naked in a creek, the corpse ignored by her husband and his friends until their fishing trip is conveniently over.

It is no coincidence, therefore, that the waitress's vision of liberation comes to her during the act of sexual intercourse. But her vision is as strange as it is unfocused and, in a sense, misdirected. "When he gets on me," she tells Rita, "I suddenly feel fat. I feel I am terrifically fat, so fat that Rudy is a tiny thing and hardly there at all." Hoping on some level to free herself of her husband's suffocating influence, her desires for liberty take the form, consciously or unconsciously, of a *literal*, physical self-expansion whose dimensions reduce the man astride her, shrinking him both in importance and size. "Surely we have diminished one another," Carver writes in a poem (the opening poem of *At Night the Salmon Move*), the complaint of another lover falling out of love.[17] In "Fat," ironically, the more diminished lover of the two — the wife — retaliates against her husband (psychically, imaginatively) in the very manner she has been abused, thus recapitulating her injuries. Reduced to the status of near-nonentity, she responds in a way that is simultaneously an adopting of Rudy's strategies and a private, uniquely personalized expression that centers and localizes diminishment at the very locus of violation: the flesh. Most vulnerable on the sexual level — what may be intimacy to one party is coercive trespass to another — the waitress transforms herself, in a vision, from non-self to mountains of self, identifying with the fat man and his determined world even as she seeks refuge from that world, at once accepting and struggling against determinism, against the complacency that imprisons.

But visions, after all, are not escape routes, and just as Carver rarely affords his characters visions, he never affords them routes of escape. The waitress's story, though it provides for her in its telling a purgation or compensation of some kind (as talking does for Carver's characters, to a degree, in all of his books), like her vision of amplitude it does little to illuminate for her the dire matter of her unhappiness. Just as the girl in "Why Don't You Dance?" keeps "talking" in an effort to get some equally disturbing details off her mind — trying in her own way "to get it all talked out" — so does the waitress of "Fat" unfold her tale. And like Rita, who "doesn't know what to make of it," and who "sits there waiting" at the end of the story, listening for some kind of interpretive nudge, the waitress remains oddly baffled in the wake of her tale, even as she is expectant about her life's forecast. "My life is going to change," she says in the final line of the story. "I feel it." (Is she intuiting the advent of pregnancy? She's just described an act of copulation and earlier had wondered "what would happen if [she] had children" — children suggesting a liberation of sorts, but also another trap, a snare.) "Her inarticulateness," as one critic notes, "stakes out the limits of her growth of consciousness"; even more significantly, her closing words extend and reinforce such limits, reflected as they are in her use of the passive construction.[18] She does not say "I am going to change my life," but "My life is going to change" — a different way of stating things. Verbal passivity is a close relative of passivity of action — it mirrors, in fact, the passive role she plays in bed — and the ultimate sense of the story's close is that the waitress will not act but will continue to be acted upon; she is programmed to see her life in those terms. Like the fat man, who admits that "A person has to be comfortable," and then, a victim of his appetite, can't stop eating long enough to remove his coat, Carver's waitress has not yet the capacity for putting on her expansive self, comfortable or uncomfortable as she may be.

A frail, mousy man wearing "slippers, pajamas, and robe," the protagonist of "Are You A Doctor?," Arnold Breit, spends many of his evenings alone while his wife, in an odd form of role reversal, is "away on business." One night his world is disrupted by a phone call from a woman whose forwardness upsets the patterned evenness of his world. As with the waitress in "Fat," his personal sense of self is threatened by sex, but in this case it is not so much sex that threatens as it is the mere potential for sexual mobility. Hence, reminding himself that "one couldn't take chances," Arnold temporarily evades the advances of the caller until, pressured into a physical confrontation, his ordeal provides less an instructive adventure than a painful destabilization of self.

Even before he is propositioned, Arnold appears insecure, hurrying as he does to the phone. He seems to feel threatened by the independence of his wife, who customarily phones "late . . . after a few drinks — each night when she [is] out of town." Arnold's insecurity is a scaled-down version of Carl's insecurity in "What's in Alaska?" which takes the shape of a pair of eyes — glowing animal eyes — that, embodying his paranoias about the future and about his girlfriend's fidelity, stalk him in a darkened hallway. Carver's protagonists are "creatures in crisis," as Michael Wood writes of this volume; the stories they inhabit, Wood concludes, are "full of menace" precisely because "The expected catastrophe, though absent as crisis or melodrama, is perpetually present as fear." [19] Like Carl and a number of others, Arnold is stalked by fear, though the embodiment of such fear is more concretely manifested for him than for some, appearing as it does in the form of Clara, the wrong number caller, who makes sexual opportunity rise suddenly like a boil on the smooth skin of his sheltered, though not necessary stable, domestic life. Similarly, in "Jerry and Molly and Sam," another male character senses that, thanks to an affair he is having, he is "losing control over everything." Likewise shaken by his caller's advances, Arnold feels his own feeble control slipping away, in this case due not to actual infidelity but to the very thought of it, and to the terrible freedom such possibility implies — a freedom which disorients, releasing one from the comfortable, entrapping bonds of marriage, and which terrifies, allowing one to imagine one's spouse capable of equal freedom.

Appropriately, the greatest erosion of Arnold's self-possession comes with the relinquishing of his name. When Clara asks him his name he replies, " 'Arnold Breit' . . . and then quickly add[s], 'Clara Holt. That's nice. But I really think I should hang up now, Miss Holt.' " Realizing that he has voluntarily turned his name over to a stranger, he tries to blot it out of her memory at once, diverting attention to her own name (which doesn't work, of course; Clara's young daughter greets him with his full name when he arrives at their door). Even more strikingly than the waitress in "Fat" — who admits that she has told Rita "too much" — Arnold spreads his already unstable sense of self dangerously thin, and, as Stull observes, tangles "his identity in a web of his own making." [20] In this progressive tangling, Arnold more than once in the story looks "at himself in the mirror" and inventories the eroding of what had been before a relatively secure self. In the final lines of the story, therefore, when the one and only exchange between husband and wife occurs, his wife says, "Arnold? . . . You don't sound like yourself."

If the lure of sexual possibility activates in Arnold what Boxer and Phillips call "dissociation" — that "sense of disengagement from one's own identity and life, a state of standing apart from whatever defines the self, or of being unselfed" — then the loss of his name figuratively recapitulates and clinches such dissociation. [21] For Arnold's dissociated cousins in the volume, psychic erosion is even more extreme. In "Collecters," Slater loses not only a letter and the possibility of a job, but also — at the mercy of the man and his vacuum — himself, a transient and precarious self signified by his name on the envelope, which is carted off with the rest of the debris, those "bits and pieces" sealed up in the bowels of the intruder's machine. In "The Father" dissociation is pushed to its expressionistic limit — the story's title figure turns to his family with a face "white and without expression," having been informed that he "doesn't look like *anybody*" (the next remove from not sounding like oneself).

In the final moments of "Are You A Doctor?" Arnold falls mute. Questioned in a joking way by his wife about his recent whereabouts, he does not respond but instead "remain[s] silent and consider[s] her voice." Arnold's silence is both an intensification and natural result of what has been building and accumulating throughout the story, at least as far as communication is concerned; his reluctant though oddly enticing conversations with Clara, particularly the one taking place in the flesh, have failed miserably, and so by extension have his attempts at communicating with himself. Now, verbal interaction with his wife, whom he doesn't seem to altogether trust, collapses. Like Rita and the talk-spent waitress, he waits; and like Leo in "What Is It?," he merely "considers," now too dissociated from himself and too alienated in general to respond in any intelligible way. He is so perturbed by the ringing of the phone (before picking it up to discover his wife on the other end) that he takes an inventory of another kind — not by looking in the mirror this time but by placing his hand "tenderly . . . against his chest" and feeling, "through the layers of clothes, his beating heart." Ineffective as the gesture may seem — most of the gestures Carver allots his characters are — Arnold's final self-inventory is significant in that as he reaches up he becomes the "doctor" of the story's title: he is trying, however awkwardly, to doctor himself. "Unselfed" by his tryst with Clara, and destabilized again by the phone, Arnold now seeks an indicator of self, however faint, and finds it.

What he finds is the "human noise" emerging out of silence at the end of "What We Talk About When We Talk About Love," that automatic idle, in the form of a heartbeat, presiding over being after the collapse of language, after dissociation is ruinously complete. Hurrying away earlier from Clara's apartment, he'd wondered about "the other child — the boy. Where was he?" Not just the story's "doctor," Arnold is also the missing boy, himself as much a point of vacancy in the story's psychic economy as the boy is a hole in the structural whole of the narrative. "I'm afraid for the boy," Clara tells him earlier in the day, just before he asks about her husband. Arnold, too, is afraid, shaken by his own ongoing and terrifying self-disintegration, a thing he is beginning to sense but cannot understand.

If Carver "cuts America's heart out," as Gary Fisketjon writes, "and lays it open in a book," then in this world of inexplicable, terrible domesticity, Arnold's fears are everybody's fears.[22] Thanks to the surgical deftness of Carver's hand, in other words, the vacuum at the center of Arnold's world represents, to greater and lesser degrees, the missing essence of us all.

In "What Is It?," one of Carver's darkest, most unsettling stories, sexuality and loss of self are linked in an even more concrete way. In this story, an insolvent man, Leo, waits at home all night in torment while his wife is out "negotiating" a deal on their convertible (and also, we presume, caps the deal by sleeping with the salesman who buys the car). Infidelity, of course, is not an unusual subject in Carver's fiction; it resounds throughout his canon as an obsession. This book treats the subject explicitly in "What Is It?" as well as in the title story and in "Jerry and Molly and Sam." Infidelity crops up again, at least indirectly, in his three other volumes of fiction: What We Talk About deals directly with the subject in "Sacks" and "Gazebo," and later volumes bring us "Fever" and "Menudo," further fantasies on this theme. In the poetry, the subject is equally if not more prevalent. In Carver (and in reality, one tends to think), infidelity manifests itself as one of many symptoms of ailing marriages and ailing selves. In "What Is It?" such dis-ease is treated more vividly than ever, reflecting the spiritual bankruptcy to which at least one marriage is prone, a marriage in which, bleak as it seems, conjugal proximity teams up with bad fortune to destroy what is left. "[B]etrayal is just another word for loss, for hunger," Carver writes, years later, in a poem.[23] In the early stories, however, sexual politics — infidelity chief among them — go beyond simply reflecting the hunger and the losses of unfortunate lovers. Such politics complicate an already complicated world, heightening the degrees of individual loss and pain. The more Carver's characters seek to recover, the more they lose.

"You don't have money," Leo's wife Toni tells him, readying herself to go out to sell the car. "And your credit's lousy. You're nothing." Although she is, as she adds, only "Teasing," she is also in earnest, considering as we must the vehemence with which she hurls "Bankrupt" at him when she returns at dawn, one of the few words, after her return, exchanged between them at all. In this rather obvious way, Leo's value as a person is reduced to his equivalency in monetary worth. He is, in the literal sense, of no account whatsoever. Himself an adulterer, Leo finds that the sight of his neighbor — a witness to the time he "brought a woman home" — fills him with an "urge to cry out a confession," and thus his wife's infidelity, which he in a perverse sense encourages ("Leo sends Toni out to do it," the story's first sentence reads), is an act of retribution he inflicts indirectly upon himself. Beyond that, Toni's infidelity is itself an embodiment of his failures — or, more precisely, a figuration of his nonexistence, in both his wife's eyes and his own. As the nightmarish aspects of his evening alone begin to wear on him, Leo "considers whether he should go to the basement . . . and hang himself with his belt. He understands he is willing to be dead." The temporary absence of his wife, underlining monetary and sexual inadequacies in equivalent terms, is a loss for him as comprehensive as it is intense; he would rather "be dead" than have to wholly confront the psychic contours of his bankruptcy. Leo's insomnia, a common malady in Carver's ecosystem of malaise (the "terrible sunrise" in "The Student's Wife" comes to mind), is a form of existential self-torment, a "wakefulness" which represents, as Boxer and Phillips observe of this story, "a particularly ineluctable sort of awakening to the tenuousness of human connections."[24] Waking to disconnectedness, Leo confronts the tenuousness of his relations with others as well as himself. Accordingly, disconcertingly, he undergoes a gradual death of self: he considers himself, in the end, "nothing."

His gradual acknowledgment of and resistance to this unpleasant awakening leads to paralysis, one that affects him both verbally and physically. After a period of interminable fidgeting, the phone rings again; Leo "looks at his hand," which "makes a fist as he watches." By this point in the story Leo's crisis is such that the motions of his body seem oddly separate, his motor reflexes exerting a control of their own. By the time his wife returns, he is angry enough to "cock his fist," ready to strike her, but — not the lion that his name connotes — he doesn't follow through with the motion. Instead, paralyzed, he allows her to tear his shirt from him and looks "for something heavy," responding to a more brutal though (fortunately for them both) equally ineffective, half-hearted impulse.

On the verbal level, Leo is more constricted yet. He utters not a word to his wife when she arrives home and fails to articulate much of anything to the car salesman when the two of them meet. In contrast to the glib verbosity of the salesman (mirroring the contrast between the salesman's "white linen suit" and Leo's tattered shirt, which he bunches "into his trousers"), Leo's verbal failure underscores his feelings of impotence, his sense of himself as a zero in both the sexual and the material realm. Tongue-tied, awkward, Leo is representative of Carver's characters in general, who, as Adam Mars-Jones says of the "walking wounded" in *What We Talk About When We Talk About Love*, "utter broken sentences and try to communicate their sense of loss," and for whom, when put to the test, "articulateness is the first thing to go."[25] For such characters, Ann Beattie writes, "Silence seems as appropriate a response as anything else."[26]

The story's title, "What Is It?" issuing from the mouth of the man who has just slept with Leo's wife, further emphasizes Leo's incapacities by drawing attention to the silence that hinders efforts toward articulation. The salesman's question, with the expectation it evokes, deflates Leo's utterance in advance. Leo's one word response, "Monday," when it comes, is a life raft of sorts, a seeming password to freedom, signifying the day (as Leo imagines) he and his wife "start over." The awkward silence enveloping Leo's statement reflects little more than the hopelessness of his hopes, the paucity of his speech mirroring that doubly speculative void in which hope, like money, is swallowed up forever. When he reissued the story in *Where I'm Calling From*, curiously enough, Carver re-titled it "Are These Actual Miles?" With the new title he adopts another of the saleman's questions — a question Leo doesn't answer. While emphasizing even more fully Leo's verbal paralysis, and by extension his failures in general, the revised title also evokes, with great explicitness, the loss that such failures imply. The "actual" miles, the story's final sentences suggest, are miles Leo's marriage has accumulated (symbolized by the "roads" in Toni's skin — a detail picking up earlier parallels between her and the car; Toni's absence is most tangible when Leo looks out the window "to the place in the drive where she always parks"). The residual toll of those miles is embodied by equal diminishment on the parts of husband and wife. Equating them both with objects and figures, the balance sheet of their marriage is dangerously overdrawn, and "Monday" — the key that Leo thinks may turn back the odometer of their misfortunes — if it ever comes, carries few promises. Materially and spiritually, Carver suggests, the forecast is not good.

In "Will You Please Be Quiet, Please?" Carver takes on the subject of infidelity again, providing a fuller psychological treatment than in any other story. Unlike "What Is It?" a story in which we see the inevitable breakdown of a broken man, this story deals with a relatively stable character. It presents an at least temporarily "happy couple," and the kind of relationship which, with the partial exception of the Millers, emerges nowhere else in the volume. In contrast to Leo, and to a host of Carver's other characters, Ralph Wyman is relatively successful and seems content with his life. Still, like a number of other males in the collection — Leo and Arnold, for instance, or Carl in "What's in Alaska?" — Ralph is oddly naive in his dealings with the female sex and is therefore vulnerable. The "only a single injury to their marriage" exists first as possibility, taking the form of what he supposes to have been an act of infidelity on the part of Marion, his wife, the "certain unthinkable particularities" of which have gnawed at him for years. When possibility is confirmed as reality — after Ralph wrings a confession out of his spouse — the sudden encroachment of the "unthinkable" upon his life destabilizes him utterly, throwing his seemingly secure identity, and his entire world, into turmoil.

In his most graphic demonstration yet, Carver illustrates how menace can lurk in the calmest of relationships for years before finally rising to the surface. More stable than any figure in this volume, Ralph is subjected to the most violent, explosive identity crisis of them all (perhaps because he, unlike others, is capable of comprehending his crisis as such). And, as we have seen again and again in Carver, the crisis hinges on sex. As the story suggests, Marion's admission releases in Ralph another self — an older and more destructive self going by the name of "Jackson," which, for the love of wife-to-be and career, he had earlier suppressed; as Boxer and Phillips observe, Ralph "has paved over, not rid himself of Jackson, the Dionysian side of him which continues to haunt his conscious mind."[27] In the bursting of Ralph's world we see, less obviously, that Marion's "threateningly mysterious sensuality" is associated in his mind with the "squalor and open lust" that appalled him years before in Mexico, where he had a disturbing "vision" of his wife, watching her secretly as she leaned against the railing of a porch. Inexplicably intimidating to him, Marion's "breasts pushing" against her blouse are for Ralph connected to the "great evil pushing at the world," that sense of uncontainability which, as his night-long drunk suggests, is both mysteriously feminine and pregnant with danger.

Ralph's fear of the uncontrollably feminine arises with sporadic intensity during his nightmarish descent into hell (an American neo-realist's version of Joyce's night-town), fear heralded before he leaves by his wife's reference to a trio of exemplary misogynists — Nietzsche, Strindberg, and Mailer — and reinforced progressively by what he sees in hell: pornographic graffiti; visions of Marion in the act of copulation; a "huge neon-lighted clam shell with a man's legs sticking out"; even the sight of a woman tossing her hair, which is as "frightening" to Ralph as anything he has ever seen. But by insisting on his wife's confession, on fueling his personal male erotic nightmare, Ralph is journeying long before he leaves, embarking early on a dangerous descent available to him in the form of language. To Marion such an activity is "just talking," but to Ralph, as the story insists, this is perilous intercourse indeed. Thus as Marion begins dishing out the meat-and-potatoes of her tale, Ralph directs "all his attention into one of the tiny black coaches in the tablecloth," where he sees that

Four tiny white prancing horses pulled each of the black coaches and the figure driving the horses had his arms up and wore a tall hat, and suitcases were strapped down atop the coach, and what looked like a kerosene lamp hung from the side, and if he were listening at all it was from inside the black coach. (234)

Riding through the dark in a coach, Ralph's imagined journey, prefiguring calamity to come on the streets of Eureka, is yet another manifestation of that "great evil" pushing at the seams of the world, and, just as significantly, a response to such evil. A wary participant, a passive listener along for the ride in a "black coach," Ralph unconsciously fashions himself the victim of "evil" coming to him in the form of language. Like Leo

— speechless in the end, helplessly "considering" — Ralph is on the road to silence, where words, and the potential horror behind words, can do him no harm. Fittingly, just before Marion begins her story Ralph admits his reservations, telling his wife he'd "just as soon leave it at that," and then tells himself that "it would be silent somewhere if he had not married." Faced with the devastating and contradictory nature of love, and its dire manifestations in discourse, Ralph, like the speaker of "This Word Love," does little more than "Listen" — then suffers for it.

Silence, then, is in a sense the antidote for bad talk. It halts and negates the circumlocutions, those nightmare journeys of potentially destructive conversation. Playing off Hemingway's line, "Will you please please please please please please please be quiet?" (borrowed from a story making a similar statement about the efficacy of talk), Carver's title, and Ralph's repetitions of it, reinforces the notion that "quiet," like sex, is a powerful restorative, counteracting to an extent the machinations of body and tongue. The bathroom, a haven for silence, provides Ralph with temporary though necessary isolation, along with the baptismal effects of water. (He partly succeeds where others have failed: Leo, acting on the same impulse, continually "splashes water on his face" but cannot purge himself of his torments; Jake Barnes, also banged up in the name of love, can't get the bath water to flow.) Ralph runs a bath and actually gets "into the water," itself a positive act and prelude to the greater act of restoration soon available to him in the form of sex. Hence Ralph finds it is "easier to let go a little," and turns to his wife, finally, after she has climbed into bed and silently placated him. "He turned and turned in what might have been a stupendous sleep," the story's last sentence reads, "and he was still turning, marveling at the impossible changes he felt moving over him." Through verbal repetition — especially of the gerund — Carver suggests the kinds of possibility residing in the "impossible," emphasizing that the road to recovery is part of the journey, too. He also suggests, ironically, that the remedy for such dis-ease lies in its cause. For Ralph and Marion, sex will now restore, at least in part, what sex has earlier undertaken to destroy.

"Love comforteth," Shakespeare writes, "like sunshine after rain." It is often the case, we should hasten to add, that love, or a version of love, is what brings the rain in the first place. "How should a man act," Ralph asks himself in his distraction, "given these circumstances?" — and then, giving in to love, answers his own question by quietly surrendering himself to that which has been eating him for so long. Ralph's compensation, embodied not only in the form of sexual intimacy but also in the possibility of acceptance and understanding, strikes an affirmative note which is rare to this volume, and which will not emerge again until *Cathedral*.[28] A light note amid a tide of darker ones, it anticipates Carver's later, somewhat more affirmative work, including his revision of "This Word Love," the last stanza of which he altered radically for inclusion in the final volume of poems:

> But this word love —
> this word grows dark, grows
> heavy and shakes itself, begins
> to eat, to shudder and convulse
> its way through this paper
> until we too have dimmed in
> its transparent throat and still
> are riven, are glistening, hip and thigh, your
> loosened hair which knows
> no hesitation.[29]

Not willing as he was in the earlier version to merely "Listen" to love's corrosion, the poem's speaker now celebrates love even as he condemns it. The lovers, swallowed and devoured in the maw of love, "are riven" even as they "are glistening," simultaneously torn apart and intimately united in the act of sex. In this sense are Ralph and Toni also "dimmed" in the "transparent throat" of love. Turning to his wife in the end, Ralph relinquishes himself, like the speaker of the poem, to something far larger than himself or his wife, far more encompassing than their petty acts and words, far greater than his fears. In doing so, Ralph is precursor to a new strain of character in Carver's canon, anticipating characters who, turning up here and there in the last two volumes, persist in their struggles almost to the point of accepting them — characters who, in rare instances, come close to celebrating their struggles, who find comfort in the small, good things of their lives and consolation in the face of an incomprehensible, unfair, brutal world.

"[T]he world is the world," says Stephen Spender, excerpted by Carver in an epigraph to a poem, "And it writes no histories that end in love."[30] Indeed, as Carver's fictive histories attest, the world and its relationships are marked more by love's absence than by love itself. Struck down by love's diseases, battered by impulses as contradictory and powerful as the disorienting world they mirror, Carver's characters are dissociated from themselves, alienated from everybody and everything they know. But despite their individual dissociations and alienations, the characters rarely surrender. "It's their lives they've become uncomfortable with," Carver says in an interview, "lives they see breaking down. They'd like to set things right, but they can't. And usually they do know it . . . and after that they just do the best they can."[31] Elsewhere, Carver says, "[I]t's really a question of enduring and abiding," speaking for his characters as well as for himself.[32] Ralph Wyman, the most articulate of Carver's early figures and mouthpiece for a number of others whose questions take the form of half-hearted gestures, endures by shutting up and acting instinctually, realizing that he "did not know what to do . . . not just in this, not just about this, today and tomorrow, but every day on earth." Archetypally a survivor, Ralph does the best he can in what is for him an unbearable, "impossible" situation: he makes love to his wife, he abides, and he endures.

Calling himself an "instinctual writer," Carver explains:

There are certain obsessions that I have and try to give voice to: the relationships between men and women, why we oftentimes lose the things we put the most value on, the mismanagement of our own inner resources. I'm also interested in survival, what people can do to raise themselves up when they've been laid low.[33]

Loss, mismanagement, survival: these are the hard cold facts of Carver's world. It should not be surprising for us, therefore, to find so many of his figures at a loss for words, to see them managing badly with the delimited vocabularies they struggle to master, or reduced to outright speechlessness. Still, silence is more than an outward expression of inner mayhem, more than a personal response, emerging on the level of language, to the chaos of phenomena. Like sex, silence can be medicinal, providing a respite from that ready-made flow of language, which often confuses already confusing circumstances more than it sorts them out.

"Talk and love run at odds," Stull writes of Carver's second book of stories, a work that is by comparison far more laconic than his first in both characterization and style, and whose title story ends with a pair of couples sitting speechless in the dark, wearied by their circumlocutions on the subject of love.[34] "Love, or be silent," Shakespeare's Cordelia observes under her breath, insisting, on a similar note, how much more ponderous love is than her tongue.

In a poem appearing nearly a decade after *Will You Please Be Quiet, Please*, Carver's speaker admits, "There was a time/I would've died for love," but adds, evoking an apocalyptically Yeatsian disorientation, "No more. That center wouldn't hold." In the last stanza of the poem, shaken by memories of old love and thoughts of death, the speaker says, "I find myself, at last, in perfect silence."[35] Lacking this degree of self-possession, Carver's early characters also "find" themselves, or at least make efforts in that direction. Arnold Breit, checking his identity for vital signs, considers his wife's voice but cannot or will not respond; Leo and Ralph, likewise silent considerers, are men whose torments, bad as they are, bring them back to the very source of their troubles — to bed — with markedly varying degrees of relief. Though more extreme, such impulses toward silence are on a par with the waitress's impulse toward talk, with her urge to share her story about the fat man: all are seeking on some level to "find" themselves (in the sense both of encountering and discovering) in the "perfect silence" of understanding, in that ideal and only vaguely imaginable realm of marital complacency where worry and jealousy and self-diminishment hold neither sway nor say. For all of these characters, however — and for most of us, whether alive in the flesh or on the printed page — such silence, such self-assurance, is impossible. But we have to admire them for trying, and to admire Carver for giving them the incentive to persist, often against great odds, in their trials.

# Chapter Two

LESS IS MORE: THE POWER OF STYLE IN *What We Talk About When We Talk About Love*

*Vita brevis est, ars longa* — Seneca

If *What We Talk About When We Talk About Love* was the book that secured Carver's reputation as a major American writer of fiction, it also brought on the mixed nature of that reputation, prompting accolades as well as suspicion, dividing reviewers and critics across the country. With the advent of *What We Talk About* Carver became, on one hand, "the greatest short story writer since Hemingway" (Robert Stone), the "godfather" of literary "minimalism" and the model for a "burgeoning school of workshop storywriters" (Robert Coover), and on the other, a "superb technician" who was "dangerous" as a "trendsetter" (Madison Smartt Bell), and whose writings represented, in the most negative sense, "the barren idiom of our time" (James Atlas).[1] Carver was decried for his "monotone," his "deadeningly sparse" verbal textures, his "impoverished language" and verbal "anorexia," even as he was lauded for his "stunning inarticulateness," for creating a voice "impregnated with the unsayable," and for the "careful starkness and understatement" of *What We Talk About*, a "minimalist masterpiece" exploring the uncanny "purity of emptiness."[2]

There is more at stake here than the perennial issues of *de gustibus*, it would seem, and more too than that age-old argument about brevity and what is and isn't the soul of wit. Greatness in art, more often than not, is linked to the threat of the new, to dangerous innovation, and Carver's work, given its freshness and oddness, is evidently more threatening than some. The sheer plenitude of terminologies arising in Carver's wake (and in the wake of Beattie and Hempel and Mason and Wolff and Ford, among others) — "neorealism," "hyperrealism," "superrealism," "existential realism," "photorealism," "catatonic realism," "dirty realism," "minimalism," "K-Mart minimalism," "Diet Pepsi minimalism," and "hick chic," to name but a few — indicates at once the novelty of the new prose and, considering the less positive classifications, the insecurity it has provoked. (John Barth's term, "Post-Vietnam, post-literary, postmodernist blue-collar neo-early-Hemingwayism," is my favorite, if only for its rhythm and humor.)[3] "Minimalism," sadly enough, seems to be the name that has stuck, not only for Carver's work but also for that of his contemporaries. The term has served in recent years as a tenacious flypaper trap ensnaring scores of writers, writers as like unto each other as airplanes and sparrows and gnats. More so than most labels, "minimalism" is an unfortunate one, mainly because it is inaccurate; the artifacts of the disciplines from which it was borrowed, music and art, bear no resemblance to Carver's work, a fact which alone renders the term inoperative. Along with many of his followers and peers, Carver found the term inappropriate and offensive when applied to his art, resented it, and rightly rejected it.[4]

The best way to understand what we talk about when we talk about Carver's style is to look searchingly into the stories themselves, to observe with a minimum of external clutter, avoiding the ready snares of terminologies as we approach the seemingly unapproachable heart of Carver's technique. What is it, we must ask at the outset, that makes these stories as powerful as they are? From whence emerges their uncannny power, capable of rousing not only small armies of critics but a major trend in American writing, making Carver (to use Robert Houston's phrase) a capital letter "Influence" just months after the appearance of his second major press book? How does Carver's style, so transparent, so sharp in places it almost pierces the skin, collaborate with his subjects, with the thematic universe of his art? How is his "terrible lucidity," as Houston calls it, "inseparable from his vision" — why terrible, and why so implacably real?[5]

As in the first volume, the characters of *What We Talk About When We Talk About Love* are bewildered in their dealings with themselves and with others, victims of the chaos which dominates their lives. In this volume, though, we see immediately that the psychic stakes have risen. While the characters of *Will You Please Be Quiet, Please?* seem primarily inert, timid, and harmless in the face of confusion, their successors in *What We Talk About* carry those earlier plights to the next remove. Intimidated now rather than timid, embittered as well as dismayed, these characters suffer in markedly new ways; many are not only numbed and confused but outraged as well, hovering precariously close to violence, and in a few cases — in "Tell the Women We're Going" and "The Third Thing That Killed My Father Off" — to murder.

In accordance with this shift, Carver's prose style, which had earlier been looser and slightly fuller, constricts as if in obeyance to his fiercer subject matter, to the thinly veiled rage of his characters. This is "Winesburg West," as it has been dubbed, a place darkened by havoc and loss, a world with little light at the end of the tunnel, or no light at all. Its darkness, rife with fear and frustration and brooding violence, is underlined and enhanced by Carver's style — his diction, his syntax and bare imagery, and the narrative strategies he employs in representing that world.[6] With Hopperesque coolness, Carver paints a disturbing picture of the "walking wounded of American suburbia," as his cast of survivors has been called; he paints a darker, more chilly America, a nation faced with limited faculties and means yet still miraculously capable of adjusting to disorder and adapting to pain.[7] He brings this picture out in ways that disarm us, revealing it in a medium whose uncanny power, for all its deceptive simplicity, its intangibility, its uniqueness, is anything but minimal.

In "Viewfinder," one of Carver's walking wounded turns up literally so in the form of a man who has lost both his hands, and who sells photographs door-to-door. The story explores the odd identification of the photographer with the narrator, who, his family having apparently abandoned him, lives alone in his house. Resonating with certain thematic concerns of *Will You Please Be Quiet, Please?* the story deals in more compressed fashion with the issue of loss, and of lost or unstable identity. And as with many stories in this volume, identification here goes beyond a simple pairing of characters: the photographer emerges in the end as a concrete manifestation of the narrator's own pain, of his own recent psychic dismemberment.[8] The narrator's denial, firmly bound up with his pain, is mirrored in the story's rhetoric and its overall narrative energies — mirrored by what is excluded in the story, and by the finer technical details of its language. Thus identification extends beyond character to the stylistic operations of discourse itself, rippling out like rings in a pond, agitating the surface of the story's language and shape.

On the most basic level things are not so different from the world of *Will You Please Be Quiet, Please?* As in Carver's first volume, vicariousness runs rampant, with character after character persistently if unwittingly gauging himself through the image of another. "I'd been watching from the window, you see," admits the narrator of "Viewfinder," referring to the handicapped man (who'd been standing outside) and to the man's awkward methods of photography.[9] But now Carver gives the screw of vicariousness another turn, suggesting that the objects of the voyeur's desires are finally their own images, a suggestion implied obliquely in the earlier volume with its profusion of mirrors and mirror-gazers. "I looked a little closer," this narrator explains, describing the photograph the man has given him, "and saw my head, *my head*, in there inside the kitchen window." From the relatively straightforward brand of vicariousness of "Neighbors," then, to the slightly more complicated version of "The Idea" (where watchers watch others watch), vicariousness evolves in "Viewfinder" to a snake-biting-its-tail point of exhaustion; as a motif it is now on the verge of collapsing into itself. Vicariousness swings full circle; the narrator scrutinizes the photo and observes himself in the act, observes observation, following it back to its source.

Contrary to watchers of earlier stories, however — whose obsessive vicariousness is grounded in vague yearnings for fuller selves — the narrator of this story is not of a yearning nature. "I wanted to see how he would hold a cup," he says at the start, having invited the photographer in for coffee. His fascination for the man, and for the man's handicap, stems not from envy, or from any typical if inexplicable craving for otherness, but from a curiosity piqued by what he senses to be their mutual likeness. He wants to see how the man has adapted to calamity. The narrator is adapting, too: he is dealing on an emotional level with what he bitterly though humorously calls a "tragedy," and in the course of the story he makes overtures toward reestablishing a focus in his life — the focus to which the story's title gives play. Thus he bids his guest take multiple photographs — photographs suggesting stasis, aptly enough, in the sense of both frozen space and time and of familial unity (portraits of family and home). Slightly more self-aware if also more detached and cynical than his predecessors, this speaker seeks himself in the viewfinder, personal stability in a destablized world. Yet in keeping with Carver's dark view of things, stability is no mere stone's throw away. "I don't do motion shots," the photographer shouts as his host hurls rocks from the roof, implying that his host may emerge in the developed photos only as the emotional blur he is at present, and perhaps has been much of his life. "It won't work," the photographer warns him early on, intuiting the circumstances: "They're not coming back." Similarly in a later story, "Vitamins," a deranged veteran named Nelson admonishes a young couple who are bewildered by their lives and who seek emotional nutrients in the compensatory way of sex. "It ain't going to do no good!" Nelson yells, echoing the man with the hooks, though even more strangely prophetic in tone and bearing; his words are indeed a hard pill to swallow: "Whatever you do, it ain't going to help none!"[10]

Heaving stones into the air and shouting, the abandoned husband of "Viewfinder" is one of a number of male characters in *What We Talk About When We Talk About Love* overcome by violence in their personal frustrations. One hurls a jar of pickles through a window while another sabotages fresh-baked pies and slashes the cord on the phone. One kills his wife with a hammer; another cudgels a pair of young women to death with a rock. Rising out of the fear and paranoia of *Will You Please Be Quiet, Please?* and mellowing later into the relative placidity of *Cathedral*, these outbursts attest to the inevitable course of buried violence in Carver's world — to the return of the repressed, and to the extremity at the heart of all conflict, and of all stories, be the violence readily visible or not. But there is more to the escapade on the roof in "Viewfinder" than the uncorking of bottled frustration and anger, which is mild here in comparison to that in other stories. It is as much an act of exhibitionism as it is an emotional vent (the photographer, understandably embarrassed, responds by checking "up and down the street"), and not unrelated to the amputee's parading of his hooks. Carver's frantic lovers and ex-lovers display their problems to the world in order to externalize those problems, advertising their grief as a kind of emotional last resort. In "Will You Please Be Quiet, Please?" for instance, Ralph tells a roomful of complete strangers in a bar about his wife's infidelity. In "Menudo" a despondent Hughes goes from yard to yard raking lawns, dramatizing the extent of his despair while the neighborhood looks on. In "Why Don't You Dance?" an abandoned husband sets a whole houseful of furniture out onto his lawn, fully and unabashedly placing the intimate details of his ruined private life in plain view of the public. Exhibitionism, in all of these cases, is a last-ditch attempt at control where control no longer exists, a means for hurling oneself voluntarily into the thick of misfortune, rather than being pulled forcibly down.

If vicariousness is one form of self-denial, then exhibitionism is another, which denies self by bowling it over with an image. (For Carver's lovers, the image is typically one of numbed, restrained desperation.) In Carver's world, both manifestations seem strangely necessary, serving as safety valves for characters who struggle along even as — or because — they deny themselves further, sidestepping confrontations with their own tenuous, precariously held together identities. And just as such denial takes place in the minds of characters, so is it replicated in Carver's narratives, and in the overall narrative energies of "Viewfinder." Buried in the story of the narrator's afternoon with the photographer is another story, the tale of the narrator's split with his family (and buried also is the tale of how the man with the hooks lost his hands, which he says is "another story"). The details of the narrator's loss are initially witheld, emerging only in the scattered intuitions of the guest, unconfirmed until the story is nearly over. ("The whole kit and kaboodle," the narrator finally admits, climbing up to the roof. "They cleared right out.") On a par with the rhetorical politics of the photographer, who smiles at his host "as if he knew something he wasn't going to tell," the narrator's politics involve keeping quiet about his misfortunes — for as long as he can, anyway. By witholding information, the story itself recapitulates the denial of the denier and, in a deeper sense, his pain. As narrative, "Viewfinder" embodies and dramatizes rhetorically the subject it sets forth to tell.

This is really nothing new in top-notch prose fiction — *The Sun Also Rises* comes immediately to mind, with all its deferrals and displacements, Jake's strategies for dealing with his "wound." But Carver has distilled the process, sharpening and tightening, withholding, taking out even more in order to add to the underside of his iceberg. The complicity of rhetorical performance and subject matter also operates naturally on the level of diction, and for this reason Carver's work is often as misunderstood as it is. In tone, "Viewfinder" is characterized by its detachment, by sympathetic, humorous terseness, by an odd verbal hardness which spotlights language as denial itself. Evoking the hard-boiled mind of its speaker, the story's tone embodies tensions between detachment and sympathy, humor and emotional pain, and plays out such tensions on the level of diction and syntax. In one of his most memorable lines, the narrator, referring to his guest's artificial hands, says, "I took a good look at those hooks." In playful Skelton-like fashion half of the words in the sentence rhyme, tempering the final word and focal point of the sentence, "hooks" — itself a small glint of linguistic horror — making catastrophe seem strangely funny. Thus do we displace our own inner turmoil through the visible turmoils of others, Carver's language seems to suggest.

On the microscopic level the story is bursting with such nuances. "Again! I screamed," the story's final sentence reads, "and took up another rock." At this moment, the only real violent one in the story, violence is evoked with sudden fury on the level of language. By far the strongest verb in an otherwise restrained verbal performance, "screamed" constitutes an explosion coinciding with an emotional release. Among other such nuances is Carver's perhaps unintentional revision of Hemingway's use of the term "good." After undergoing an elaborate procedure to climb onto the roof, the speaker finds himself standing atop his house at last, and says, "It was okay up there on the roof." Revising Hemingway's motto "It was good" — applied with incantatory repetition in Nick Adams' healing retreats into the wilderness — the abandoned husband's statement suggests in one small, ordinary word that for Carver the romantic core at the center of Hemingway's modernist vocabulary is now officially dead. We may indeed have to settle for "okay," Carver implies; some of us have never known anything else, if we have been even that lucky. Recovery may not, all things considered, be as plausible a notion as it used to be. "'Ready?'" the narrator calls out from the roof, rock in hand, waiting as the man below steadies his image in the viewfinder. "'Okay!'" the man with the hooks calls back, a response that, for all its seeming simplicity, its minimality, hits exactly the right note.

In 1981, the year *What We Talk About When We Talk About Love* appeared, Carver published, "On Writing," his only essay on the mechanics of fiction. Explaining his predilection for short stories that afford "some feeling of threat or a sense of menace," he writes:

> What creates tension in a piece of fiction is partly the way the concrete words are linked together to make up the visible action of the story. But it's also the things that are left out, that are implied, the landscape just under the smooth (but sometimes broken and unsettled) surface of things.[11]

In "Viewfinder," such a "landscape" exists as the buried matter of one man's "tragedy," which though largely "left out" emerges gradually in scattered pieces, if only as a series of hints. In "Why Don't You Dance?," on the contrary, the buried matter of another's man all but identical tragedy never surfaces at all. Noticeably more radical in its suppression of detail, this story leaves the reader to surmise about its central character, a man who has inexplicably set his furniture and household items, even his lamps and stereo, on the lawn and driveway in front of his house.[12] Surveying the residual objects of his former married life, we assume that here is another of Carver's survivors, one more exhibitionistic than most; we assume, too, that like the cars passing by, full of staring onlookers that don't stop, "he [won't], either" — that he will survive in his own, however peculiar, way. As in "Viewfinder," the desperation and emotional denial of the man is underscored by the operations of narrative, mainly by omission and deferral, and by the story's diction, complicit as it is in evoking the minds of its figures.

In "Why Don't You Dance?," Carver's prose is even more terse and detached, so cool and rock-hard, so deliberately flat, that it comes across, as a reviewer says of the book's style in general, "as sparingly clear as a fifth of iced Smirnoff."[13] Operating in the omniscient perspective, the rhetoric of this story evokes here more than anywhere else the chilly, hardened state of its protagonist's mind, and does so relentlessly, beginning with an extensive survey of the man's belongings outside on the driveway and lawn; the cool blankness of the description, in all its inventorying factuality, reflects the emotional denial of the objects' owner, who had until recently viewed the objects as shared property. The voice of the story, in other words, infected by the consciousness of its central figure, reflects and enhances a sense of the man's bitterness and cynicism. Thus the unseen narrator oddly mimics himself (or herself) in describing the objects that once occupied customary sides in the bedroom ("His side, her side"); thus he or she later takes on the emotional resonances of the man, when the "preposterous question" of money comes up regarding the desk.

One of the first things his guests do when they arrive is flop down on the bed — ironically a place that was reserved in former times for the greatest intimacies, and which is now reduced to the kind of lurid public display we have seen elsewhere, a flaunting of intimacy long dead and gone. Lying on the man's bed, dancing to his records in the driveway, the young couple provides both an outlet through which the man may displace his denial (as the photographer does for his host in "Viewfinder") and a living refiguration of his marriage in its infancy, the memory of which he is now attempting to cast off. The nuances of such refiguration, accordingly, come across in the submerged tensions of the couple's conversation, not to mention in the flinty hardness of the prose:

"How is it?" he said.
"Try it," she said.
He looked around. The house was dark.
"I feel funny," he said. "Better see if anybody's home."
She bounced on the bed.
"Try it first," she said.
He lay down on the bed and put the pillow under his head.
"How does it feel?" she said.
"It feels firm," he said.
She turned on her side and put her hand to his face.
"Kiss me," she said.
"Let's get up," he said.
"Kiss me," she said.

*She closed her eyes. She held him.*
*He said, "I'll see if anybody's home." (5)*

In the most obvious sense, the boy and girl are symbolic stand-ins for the couple who bought the bed and shared it before. Less obviously, their conversation betrays tensions in their own relationship, hinting at tensions which may or may not have precipitated the break up of the older couple — most visible in the girl's eager sexual overtures and in the boy's reluctance to act in a potentially embarrassing way. The tensions here, filling the interstices of a conversation they conduct lying down, of all places, on a bed, are grounded in sexual politics. The swelling of the girl's aggressiveness — evidenced more concretely later as she interrupts her boyfriend to bargain with the man, and as she asks the man to dance — suggests that her host's present circumstances (due, perhaps, to a headstrong wife and his own stubbornness) may be a preview of the young couple later on, long after they have acquired the unhappy articles of this man's marriage.

Less obviously yet, the mechanics of the dialogue take these suggestions to an extreme. In this one half-page exchange on the bed, Carver employs sixteen pronouns — most of them forms of "he said" and "she said" — carrying to extremity what has come to be considered a trademark (and much imitated) aspect of his craft. On the most rudimentary level, such narratorial markers serve as deft rhetorical jabs, disrupting with almost irritating consistency the natural rhythm of voice and breath, thus undercutting the traditionally "poetic" potential of what in Carver's ecosystem of down-and-outers are sometimes terribly unpoetic scenes. Further, the rhetorical insistence of "he said" and "she said" also underlines the event of speech and its shortcomings, a major concern in all of Carver's books, particularly this one. It draws still further attention to the act of narration — to the way that the unique post-postmodern brand of alienation Carver's characters suffer also informs his narratives (a subject for another investigation altogether). Most important, however, these markers are assertions of personal identity — or, better, are deliberately awkward gestures in that direction. In the course of the story we learn nothing of the young couple; we are ignorant of who they are, of what they dream about and where they are going. Coupled with such noninformation, the repeated assertions of identity coming in the form of pronouns promote nonidentity more than they do identity, much less full or stable selves. Thus Carver's dance of the pronouns, a curious kind of club-foot shuffle, plays out on the level of language an identity crisis embodied metaphorically in the machinations of his central figure (who is much more a cypher than either one of the kids). "We thought nobody was here," the boy explains awkwardly when the man arrives, his words ringing with more truth than he can imagine. Pulling out his checkbook to pay for the items he buys, the boy says, "I'm making it out to cash," unwittingly equating his host with the monetary worth of his domestic goods, the accumulated baggage of a life that the man now deems utterly and irreversibly worthless.

In the final brief segment of this frayed narrative (a narrative composed of the mutually intertwining perspectives of the man and the young couple), the story favors the girl as it had earlier favored the man. With this shift in perspective, a final comment provides us with something new: a confirmation of the man's worthlessness, now through the eyes of the girl. We are obliged to consider retroactively the narrator's comments about the young couple's expressions, the looks on their faces after they've bargained with him. "It was nice or it was nasty," the man says early on. "There was no telling." They are indeed "nice" kids, the story seems to suggest, and yet they are also eager to exploit circumstances, like vultures carrying off pieces of a dead animal, fattening on disaster. While the girl lacks the intuitive powers of the photographer in "Viewfinder" — she hasn't experienced much yet in the way of hard knocks — she is nevertheless vaguely sensitive to the man's desperation: twice she refers to him as "desperate," the second utterance taking on a more informed aura. Like the waitress in "Fat," she is attuned to concerns that, though larger than her own understanding, seem to apply directly to herself. She likewise voices her concerns, trying to articulate the connection, to "get it all talked out."

In the end, then, the man's story is her story as well as a story about the man, herself, and the boy — one that heightens our sense of both "nasty" insensitivity and nicer curiosity, of exploitation and awkward sympathy, and of the way forebodings can spell out emotional wreckage to come. Appropriately, the wild card in the shuffle of final details Carver lays on the table takes the form of the "record-player" the man gives his guests, along with the "crappy records," as the girl describes them. Innocuous as it might at first seem, this small detail zeroes in on the central concerns of the story: the fathomless nature of the man's bitterness, for all his restraint, and the sorry shallowness of the boy and girl. In a last-minute flourish we are given back a detail which, as in all good, threatening stories, had been withheld. With such flourishes, as one reviewer puts it, Carver ultimately "keeps more than he abandons." [14] As a result we come away from this and other stories not so much with ready meanings but with lessons in reading. Encouraged to look deeply into the stories of others, we learn to read our own more fully and carefully, side-stepping calamities of the future if we can, or at least steeling ourselves for what we cannot avoid.

The fullest story in the collection, ironically, is a story about a man incapable of speech. "The Third Thing That Killed My Father Off" is about what "the wrong kind of women can do to you," to use the words of the narrator's father. But unlike "Viewfinder" and "Why Don't You Dance?" which explore the aftermath of such interactions, this story charts the course of a man's undoing, step by step. Worse off than many of Carver's lot, the story's central figure lacks both a name — Dummy being his nickname — and the capacity for normal self-expression. Unable to articulate himself in conventional ways, unable to get things "talked out," Dummy displaces his concerns, chief among them his fears of his wife's infidelity. He stocks a pond with black bass, and keeps vigil over the fish as he cannot seem to do with his wife. Dummy's fishpond, and the electric fence that surrounds it, is yet another manifestation of the exhibitionist impulse in Carver's world. The exhibition ends, thanks to the return of the repressed and a hammer, with Dummy murdering his wife, and with the spectacle of Dummy himself, suicidally drowned and later fished from his pond (where fishing, humorously enough, is strictly forbidden).

As with other stories, "The Third Thing" relies for much of its rhetorical power on strategies mirrored in the events and details of the story. Like "Sacks," "The Calm," and "Everything Stuck to Him" in this volume, and like "Where I'm Calling From" in the next, "The Third Thing" is a frame tale utilizing several narrative layers. Such layers displace the central impact of the story, much in the way Dummy displaces anger about his wife — anger altogether unarticulated in "Dance," restrained until the end in "Viewfinder," and exploding in this story with unusual energy and violence. Simultaneously encompassing three independent sets of concerns, "The Third Thing" is as much the narrator's story, and the narrator's father's story, as it is Dummy's; the narrative layers intersect thematically, linked by strands of the immediate tale, in which Dummy figures as primary.

"From what I hear," one of Jack's father's friends says, referring to Dummy's new fish and the precautions he takes to protect them, "he'd do better to put that fence round his house." Dummy, however, devotes more and more of himself to the pond, in the course of the story, trying in his own way to "husband" nature, which proves impossible with the coming of heavy rains. (The river, it is worth noting, is distinctly female in its intractability and uncontrollability: "She's up to fifteen feet," Jack's father says of the flooding river, monitoring her rise in the newspaper; in one version of the story — entitled "Dummy," appearing four years earlier in *Furious Seasons* — the river is referred to in the same sentence as "it's.") [15] Among other things, Dummy's tale is about the futility of trying to control the uncontrollable, and about the ways one compensates for failure, an issue mirrored in the tale of Jack's father, within which it is immediately framed.

"I'll tell you what did my father in," Jack says in the first sentence of the story. "The third thing was Dummy, that Dummy died. The first thing was Pearl Harbor. And the second thing was moving to my grandfather's farm near Wenatchee. That's where my father finished out his days, except they were probably finished out before that." Like Dummy, Jack's father knows disorder: he has seen it manifested in his life most recently in the form of a murdering, suicidal friend, and earlier in a threat to national security (a surprise attack) and in his necessary acceptance of poverty's strictures, prompted as he was to move home as a middle-aged man. Jumbling the symptoms of his father's undoing (perhaps reflecting the disoriented nature of his father's reasoning), Jack emphasizes the extent to which havoc in one's life breeds displacement, to which it can cause one to seek someone or something to blame, even if, as his father's displacements attest, the blame rests finally with oneself, or with nobody.

What is at stake for Jack in the unfolding of his father's tale, and of his father's friend's tale, is far from readily apparent. One of Jack's concerns is certainly his horror at having seen a corpse fished from the pond, the corpse of a man he knew. "It's not him," Jack says as the men pull the "dripping thing" into the boat. "It's something else that has been in there for years." Jack's denial of the horror in his recollection suggests that denial is still with him. Like that "something else" he imagines briefly, a vague substitute for the true object of horror, the ponderousness of this denial resides in him even now, having similarly been "in there for years." Beyond fishing up a youthful trauma, Jack's act of telling also attempts to come to grips with his father's dissolution — with the destabilizing of the authority figure of his childhood. "I don't think Dad really believed it," Jack says, reflecting on his father's comments about what "women can do to you," adding, "I think he just didn't know who to blame or what to say." Jack's "thinking" implies he is still searching for answers, that he is learning that the third thing is just one of many things that killed off his father, some of which he is only now beginning to fathom. Thus like his father, who displaces immediate concerns, blaming himself and women and fish and air attacks for defeats in his life, Jack likewise displaces not only a grisly spectacle of his boyhood but also lingering questions and concerns about his father, cushioning them in the protective layers of his narrative.[16]

Jack's central concern is buried deepest in these layers and is glimpsed only in the interstices of the story's weave, or — to make things easier — in an earlier version of the story. Inserted between what will eventually become the opening paragraphs of the later story, the second paragraph of "Dummy" originally read:

For me, Dummy's death signalled the end of my extraordinarily long childhood, sending me forth, ready or not, into the world of men — where defeat and death are more in the natural order of things.[17]

Because the literal references to Jack's transition in "The Third Thing" are unspoken, are in effect buried, his residual yearnings — because they are "left out," a la Hemingway — seem all the more powerful. Despite the increased hardness of the later story, the original emotional core remains, conveying in rather more subtle fashion Jack's hard-boiled nostalgia, his craving for the relative tranquility predating an adulthood where instability and heartbreak have become standard fare. Also edited out of "The Third Thing" is a passage in "Dummy" describing the "terrified" reaction of Jack's father at seeing the corpse's arm emerge from the water. Jack sees the arm as a "mysterious and terrible signal," a "herald" of his family's pending misfortunes. In the concluding sentences of the story, however, Jack qualifies his statements, saying,

But that was an impressionable period, from twelve to twenty. Now that I'm older, as old as my father was then, have lived a while in the world — been around some, as they say — I know it now for what it was, that arm. Simply, the arm of a drowned man. I have seen others.[18]

In the later version, Carver not only offers us less about the significance of the "arm" ("That arm going up and going back down in the water, it was like so long to good times and hello to bad"), but also witholds his narrator's mature reaction to it. He leaves us with a bare image only, and the sense of a young man's horror, which he deftly plays down. Suppressing the mild bitterness of the early description, Carver lets his speaker's sentiments rise in a much more refractory way: in the bitterness of Jack's father, and overall detachment of the narrative voice.

This is not by any means to say that the voice of "The Third Thing" is as detached as in most of the stories in What We Talk About, despite the excisions it underwent ("Dummy" is fuller by one-third). The voice typical to the collection bespeaks a consciousness that has seen far too many drowned men, a voice that in inarticulate near-despair admits, as does Duane in "Gazebo," that "There was this funny thing of anything could happen now that we realized it had."[19] Comparable in tone only to "Nobody Said Anything" in Will You Please Be Quiet, Please? and to a handful of stories in Furious Seasons, "The Third Thing" is more generous than any other story in What We Talk About, perhaps due in part to its anecdotal, episodic nature. Inherent in Jack's tonal range is at once a wistful longing for the securities of childhood and a seasoned, obdurately knowledgeable awareness of disorder and death; it is a voice embodying subtle tensions in tone, between soft memories of the past and the hard facts of the present. With all its displacing layers, its narrative sleight-of-hand, its stories within stories, "The Third Thing" reveals how we employ stories in the interest both of understanding and of protecting ourselves from understanding too well. Through its tonal nuances, Jack's story reveals how well our own voices, in telling such stories, reflect the inconsistency and mutability of the world those stories represent, along with the miraculous flexibility of the voice, and of the mind, for comprehending and articulating the irreconcilable.

One of the more revolutionary aspects of Carver's work is that he alters Aristotle's dictum, "to use metaphor is to see resemblance" — at least in terms of degrees of resemblance, and in terms of insisting his readers see what he sees.[20] Bald and bare as they are, Carver's metaphors refute resemblance even as they seem to assert it, with likeness toned down to the point of denial. Such metaphors, metaphorically speaking, are like guideposts set in a desert, with few discernable adjoining paths to give them — or give readers — bearing or reference. From the beginning we find in Carver a resistance to the meaning-full image. The fat man in "Fat," as pivot of the story's metaphorical energies, remains in the end almost as much a mystery to us as to the waitress, who can't get him out of her head. The shining convertible crops up intermittently in "What Is It?" as an emblem of material loss, but only in the most unassuming of ways; the car is just there (and then it is gone). Similarly, in "Nobody Said Anything" a sickly green steelhead, nebulously tied to family disintegration, a chief concern in the story, is cut in half Solomon-wise with a knife by the narrator and brought home, and while the fish tends to glow with tentative meaning, Carver the author chooses not to spell it all out.[21]

In later stories, despite swelling length and a general rhetorical loosening, image and metaphor come across nearly as drained and blank as before: the peacock in "Feathers" is simply a bird, strikingly nonradiant, connected as it seems to a glimpse of the good life; in "Preservation," a story about a marriage in the process of wilting, a broken icebox is mainly just a machine in need of replacement, despite its metaphorical aura; the cathedral in "Cathedral," likewise, is just something one might see on late-night TV.[22] Whatever connections are to be made, Carver implies, we must make for ourselves. Following Flannery O'Conner and Hemingway, for whom a big two-hearted river is a river first and foremost, and to whom a wooden leg is finally an empty, innocuous object, Carver refuses to manhandle materials, to coerce images into being something too much more than what they actually are. Objects appear and reappear in the stories, Marc Chénetier writes, as "unexplained and disquieting symptoms"; "[a]ll hollow spots" in Carver's texts, accordingly, "must be invested by the reading mind in sympathy or solidarity" with the characters and their various quandaries.[23]

In *What We Talk About When We Talk About Love*, Carver's sparest, most elliptical volume, we work harder than ever connecting meaning to image, and to what — occasionally — we take to be metaphor. Gazebos, fishponds, and slugs loom, starkly and disconcertingly appropriate but somehow always disattached in the end, at least in terms of traditional frameworks of meaning. Sprinkled with characteristically bare images and a single bare metaphor, "After the Denim" simultaneously demonstrates and justifies Carver's unwillingness to deal in such frameworks, to exploit artistic convention, to play the heavy hand with resemblance. In this story, as in many, Carver sets up a trope without binding the metaphorical strands tightly together. In this instance he also indirectly dramatizes his personal relation as author to the landscapes he creates, and to the characters that people his fiction.

"After the Denim" is about an older couple's night on the town. It is atypical only in that these characters, the Packers, share a kind of genuine intimacy, however restrained or awkward it may seem at the beginning. The Packers attend a bingo game, which is for James Packer disrupted in a double sense — first by the intrusion of a young hippy couple (one of whom James discerns to be cheating), then by the revelation of his wife's illness and, perhaps, the encroaching threat of her death. A retired accountant, James is obsessed with order and accountability, which explains his dislike for the newcomers: he can't quite account for them. The long-haired intruder doesn't "have sense enough to look after his own numbers," James figures; afterwards he puts "two and two together," seeing the couple climb into their van.

Appropriately enough, the bingo game serves as the story's master trope, sketchy as it is (and they always are in Carver's fiction). Its metaphorical glow permeates the story in a tentative, nonimperious way, playing up thematic issues of order and randomness, fairness and unfairness, good luck and bad. Early on James belabors his "lousy luck" in playing at bingo, and later, indirectly, in playing at life, particularly concerning his wife's health. It seems unfair to him that a pair of young unknowns should walk off with the jackpot, and unfair that his wife may be dying. For James there is a kind of terrible arbitrariness at work all around, with no moral or logical pattern to dictate winning and losing.

The story's images collaborate, as we might expect, with the central metaphorical drift. A "damaged street lamp" and a tree are shaken by wind, and a man in a photo stands on the overturned hull of his boat, battered — like the tree and the lamp — by unpredictable forces of nature. On levels other than visual, the chill of "[c]old air" blowing out from the refrigerator, and the sound of "surf breaking on the rocks" heighten the overall effect, contributing to the metonymic flood of detail feeding the whole — a sense of objects and people exposed, vulnerable in a world they cannot control. Even the products of James's imagination enhance the effect. The bingo beans clenched in his hand remind him of "a boy who'd thrown some beans out a window," beans that sprout in the readerly mind into a towering beanstalk, one which, unlike street-lamps and trees, leads upward into a heaven of riches (and danger, in the form of a giant).

"The proper time for using metaphor," Longinus declares — in meta-phorical fashion — "is when the passions roll like a torrent and sweep a multitude of them down their resistless floods." [24] Unlike Longinus and a host of others, Carver is not only unwilling to fully flesh out a metaphor but also is most suspicious when passions are rolling, preferring to let voiceless anxiety speak. Sitting with eyes closed in front of the silent TV, "branches whining in the birch tree behind the house," James begins to let go a little, and, for a single brief moment in the story, the rhetoric swells. "If only they had to sit with him in the waiting room!" James ex-claims to himself, referring to the young couple, and the impending visit to the doctor:

*He'd tell them what to expect! He'd set those floozies straight! He'd tell them what was waiting for you after the denim and the earrings, after touching each other and cheating at games."* (77)

The uncanny force of this verbal eruption, coupled with the peculiar, al-most poetic softness of the final sentence, spells out both the degree of James's outrage and the extent of his futility, his utter impotence in the face of chaos. What we end up with here, however, is a sea-horde rather than a tightly bound bundle of meaning ("earrings" hearkening back to the "gold hoop" in the young man's ear, related to James's own "hoop," with which, curiously feminized, he embroiders; "touching" being something James and Edith do throughout the story themselves, culminating in their final embrace, with James "awkward and terrified . . . more or less holding his wife"; setting "floozies straight" being the natural inclination of an accountant, who continually lines things up in columns), the title flung haphazardly into the rhetorical flood of this seahorde, a title which seems to unify the story only on an emotional level.

Reflecting James's mindset, then, Carver lets the outrage flow momentarily but resists the temptation to sum up, in spite of Longinus, and in spite of Wellek and Warren, who claim "image and metaphor" to be "the most centrally poetic of all stylistic devices."[25] Carver in effect just says no to poetry — or better, to forced or forcible unity, and to authorial attempts to pull together a world that, for his own characters and more than once for himself, seems hopelessly out of control. What is finally central to Carver's stories are the trials of his characters, and the less metaphorically unified, the less thematically stylized they seem as representations, the more stark and more vital those trials come across in the end. To be true to himself and his figures, Carver backs off. His art rejects traditional unity to the extent that it rejects the philosophy in which metaphor is grounded in general. In Winesburg West, in this perilously unstable world of Carver's survivors, extended metaphor implies a kind of stability, a tangible unity of vision and awareness, that if applied too deliberately would come off as worse than inaccurate: it would be false.[26]

Thus it is fitting that the metaphorical threads of "After the Denim" unravel themselves even as the textual fabric spreads out. Bingo is itself paradoxical, formalizing as it does disorder and chance, with numbers falling randomly out of a basket to correspond to tidy rows on a card. As metaphor it denies the metaphorical impulse, that tendency toward resemblance, logical similarity, and likeness, toward wholeness; bingo is both metaphor and antimetaphor, unifying the story in the broadest of ways while suggesting simultaneously that unity does not and cannot exist. By underscoring with paradox the hard facts of an alienating, unpredictable world, Carver makes a hard place seem that much more terribly hard. At the same time, he demonstrates a desire to render his world clearly and faithfully. "Fundamental accuracy of statement is the ONE sole morality of writing," Ezra Pound writes — a quip that Carver kept on a card taped over his desk, and frequently cited.[27] Technique, in this sense, is a test of sincerity.

Like James Packer, pushing his knitting aside in favor of the tools of embroidery — weaving being of course the task of the Fates — Carver embroiders his texts with image and metaphor, adding superficial yet crucial bits of color and texture to already prefabricated cloth. In the story's last moments he gives us James Packer working "stitch after stitch" into the night, compensating for hard knocks, waving off adversity like the man on the boat, looking straight into the viewfinder. Carver gives us the petty toils of quiet desperation, of a man stabbing away at fate. In doing so, here and elsewhere, he endeavors to "cleanse and revivify metaphor," as Cleanth Brooks writes of Donne, but Carver does so even more thoroughly, with more intensity of purpose.[28] Selecting, eradicating, sharpening, deliberately refusing to complete all the stitches, Carver weaves a distinctly new kind of text, and in the process effects a radical housecleaning, one altering conceptions of metaphor in fiction for good.

"Style is metaphor," Thomas Le Clair writes, referring to Carver and his contemporaries.[29] In light of our increasing awareness of Carver's artistry, the truth of this statement is only too apparent. With his nuances of diction, his omissions and deferrals and displacements, his anti-metaphorical metaphors, Carver demonstrates how intrinsic an artist's style can be to his vision — especially in *What We Talk About When We Talk About Love*, which he admits to be his most stylized volume:

The stories in What We Talk About are different to an extent [than earlier ones]. For one thing, it's a much more self-conscious book in the sense of how intentional every move was, how calculated. I pushed and pulled and worked with those stories before they went into the book to an extent I'd never done with any other stories.[30]

Carver cut his "words to the bone" in this volume, he says elsewhere, but adds that he is always careful to "leave a few slivers of meat on them."[31]

Perhaps distrustful of this kind of pushing and pulling — still hungry after a meal of slivers — Carver's detractors not only want more text for their money but also seem to resent Carver for the ways (they say) he "dictates" over his world, likening his characters to "rats negotiating a maze," puppets driven by merciless authorial will.[32] What such critics unfortunately fail to see is the distinction between a fictive world dominated by an authoritarian creator and the *representation* of such a world, a dark world where insurmountable responsibility and self-limitation are two sides of one coin and failure is a daily fact of existence. Hardly a puppetmaster, Carver is both sympathetic and implacable in his representations. Like God in Milton's cosmos, bestowing freedom of choice on his creatures, Carver affords his characters liberty to act as they might, and though they are rather worse off than Adam and Eve in the garden, his characters are necessarily more circumscribed in their choices. They exist in a fictive universe that is, like many parts of the world it reflects, fundamentally lacking in individual freedoms, be they motivated internally or externally — a place where the plot of one's life, and freedom itself, is largely determined.

Carver was always averse to plotting, in fact. In "On Writing" he reveals that his composing practices are like those of Flannery O'Connor, who "often did not know where she was going when she sat down to work on a short story."[33] He prefers to see life develop organically in fiction, to let "things to operate on their own," as he explains in an interview, "as they so often do in life."[34] If Carver's characters ultimately seem dominated, it is due not to authorial manipulativeness on Carver's part but to his willingness to reproduce a world where domination and alienation are reigning phenomena — not to mention his willingness to render that world without irony, never at the expense of his characters, or of humanity. However highly crafted they seem, Carver's stories are as respectful of as they are faithful to his world, if for no other reason than his membership in it, for his continuing allegiance to the figures that make it up. "Essentially, I am one of those confused, befuddled people," Carver admits. "I come from people like that, those are the people I've worked with and earned my living beside for years."[35] Like the amputee in "Viewfinder" — who has had more than his share of hard times but still finds room in his heart to offer sympathy to others — Carver in effect says "I sympathize," and casts his sympathy in nonironic, if coolly objective prose. So far is he from dictating to his characters that he claims to do so would be worse than insulting a friend of the family: "I have to care for the people in the stories," he says. "These are my people. I can't offend them, and I wouldn't." [36]

Yet out of the freedom of original creative expression, and out of profound sympathy, comes Carver's terrible realism, presumably shaped by the pushing and pulling and reworking that revision entails, a tinkering for which Carver more than once expressed fondness. With his signature style Carver hyperextends realism, pushing it to its barest extreme, and as a result — particularly in *What We Talk About When We Talk About Love* — he makes an oppressive, inhospitable world seem that much less expansive, that much less hospitable. Overall Carver's technical wizardry relies not so much on images and words as on their lack, and on the chill we sense in their absence. "Carver's art," Claude Richard writes, while drawing on "the best of Hemingway and certain successes of precisionism, makes one feel the force of the paradox that ensures that the deepest anxiety is, precisely, that which does not let itself speak." [37]

Blankly and terribly real, bordering on expressionism, Carver's stories explore the dark reality of a world within a world, and evoke, at the same time, the expression of an era. "Prose is architecture," Carver says, citing Flaubert. "And this isn't the baroque age." [38] With its lean scaffolding and hard internal fibers, Carver's fiction cuts away the excesses of our immediate postmodern past even as, informed by that era, it retains and intensifies the undercurrent of uneasiness that characterizes this past. Equal parts innovation and cultural testimony, *What We Talk About* is, as Jayne Ann Phillips observes, "a book of fables for this decade" — a book that, for all its disarming simplicity, shooting for maximal effects with a minimum of visible apparatus, alters our old notions of style and artistic convention, of realism, of the parameters of the American short story, and of the short story abroad. [39]

# Chapter Three

INSULARITY AND SELF-ENLARGEMENT IN *Cathedral*

In "The Compartment," one of Carver's bleakest stories ever, a man passes through the French countryside in a train, en route to a rendezvous with a son he has not seen for many years. "Now and then," the story's narrator says of the man, "Myers saw a farmhouse and its outbuildings, everything surrounded by a wall. He thought this might be a good way to live — in an old house surrounded by a wall." [1] Due to a last minute change of heart, Meyers chooses to stay insulated in his "compartment" and remain on the train, reneging his promise to the boy and walling out everything external to his selfish world, paternal obligation included.

Myers's tendency toward insularity is not unique to characters, either in *Cathedral* or in earlier volumes. The paranoid individual self-cloisterings of Slater and Arnold Breit in *Will You Please Be Quiet, Please* and the motel barricade of Holly and Duane in *What We Talk About When We Talk About Love*, among other examples, anticipate the even more dire forms of insularity we find in Carver's third major-press collection of stories. [2] In "Preservation," a man "terminated" by his employer confines himself all but completely to his living room, reclining day and night on the couch, watching TV and reading about a petrified man in a "peat bog." In "Careful," another man (from beginning to end in Carver, men are by and large the weaker, more vulnerable species) steadfastly refuses to leave his small attic garret where, clad in pajamas for most of the day, hemmed in by four walls and a roof, he has to "stoop" to keep from hitting his head on the ceiling.[3] More vividly here than in previous volumes, Carver's figures seal themselves off from the world, walling out threatening forces even as they wall themselves in, retreating destructively into the claustrophobic inner enclosures of self. In several stories, however, perhaps in response to these new extremes of insularity, we find equally striking instances where, pushing insularity the other way, characters attempt to throw off the entrapping nets and, in a few cases, almost succeed. In *Cathedral*, and in *Cathedral* only, we witness rare moments of near self-disenfranchisement, occasional bright openings in closed-down lives, however temporary those openings may be.

In Carver's world, obviously, liberation is not a thing one finds and secures on one's own. It necessarily involves the influence or guidance of a fellow being, a baker or an elderly babysitter or a blind man — even a fellow drunk on the road to recovery — who, entering unexpectedly into one's life, affords new perspective or awareness to help one along, leading one, if not toward insight, then at least away from the confining strictures of self. Such interventions and influences, as a rule, are mobilized in the stories through communal gestures of language, through exchanging tales and through other transactions, where separate identities blend and collaborate rather than collide. Thus even as "Carver's task is to depict," as Paul Skenazy writes, the "tiny, damning confinements of the spirit," his task is also to go beyond depicting the suffocations and wilted spirits of characters in chains, at least in this book.[4] Moving toward what Irving Howe calls "a greater ease of manner and generosity of feeling," engaging in what Carver himself called a writerly "opening up," Carver illustrates here and there in this book the momentary gratifications one experiences when, however temporarily, the enclosing walls come down: when self-preoccupation begins to dissolve and new freedoms appear, freedoms one may or may not truly participate in at all.[5]

Since outright freedom is for many of Carver's lot as terrifying as total lack of mobility (Arnold Breit in "Are You A Doctor?" comes to mind, as does Lloyd in "Careful") the freedoms Carver's newly liberated characters experience manifest themselves, ironically, as forms of enclosure, ample and humane as those enclosures may be. Be they comforting memories of one's old bedroom, a warm, fragrant bakery, or a vision of a cathedral's interior, they are enclosures nevertheless. Hoping to disentangle themselves from the fetters of insecurity and addiction, Carver's characters expand both inwardly and outwardly, and thanks to the beneficial incursions of other lives and other stories, they imagine larger, more spacious enclosures, places big enough and light enough to allow the spirit room to breathe — places where, as for J. P. in "Where I'm Calling From," a man can patiently "figure out how to get his life back on the track." Hence even while Carver insulates his figures more darkly than ever he also lightens his universe, a trend which continues with each new story he writes. Within our shared stories, he suggests in *Cathedral* — by means of our overtures toward human connection — we sometimes can and do set aright our derailed lives; sometimes, if we are lucky, we gain unprecedented awareness as well, awareness of our collective confinement, if nothing else, of how together we are in our perpetual aloneness.

"Chef's House" is the story of a man "on the wagon," the failure or success of whose recovery from alcoholism depends, in his mind at least, upon the borrowed home in which he is staying. Not unhappily out of work, voluntarily cut off from the world (they don't "have a telephone"), Wes and his wife Edna are more positive versions of Holly and Duane in "Gazebo," who lock themselves up in their motel out of sheer desperation, and in the process lock themselves in with their problems. Nevertheless, positive as "Chef's House" seems at the outset, and despite Wes's uncharacteristically keen sense of what he lacks, the outcome of this story, is typically grim: Wes loses his refuge, that sanctuary of his fragile recovery, along with, we presume, his tenuous battle against drink.

Even though Edna, the story's speaker, is doubtful ("I knew better," she says), their summer together is uncharacteristically nice. Enveloped in the comforts of an all but rent-free enclosure, bowled over by the charm of the place, she finds herself "wishing the summer wouldn't end." Chef's house and environs, for both Edna and Wes, is an unbelievable haven, a northern California resort on the sea as well as an Eden of sorts, a place where, given its beauty and quiet serenity, they might "start over," as Wes says early on, trying to persuade his estranged wife to share in his luck. Wes and Edna do little more all summer than fish and shop and go to the movies, enjoying the leisurely life, the "fruit juice" they drink nourishing them in the wake of disaster, reviving an earlier Eden (years before, Wes had flung his wedding ring into a "peach orchard," the last fallen fruit in a fallen-apart marriage). A pseudo-newlywed husband again, Wes takes his wife "in his arms," quaintly asking if she's "still his girl," and brings home flowers and gifts, carrying on in general like a teenager, or a child in the garden — certainly not like a figure in Carver's earlier work.

Equally striking is the brief taste we get of the outside, of nature (Carver's stories typically take place indoors). We hear of "freshwater lagoons" and of "clouds passing overhead toward the Central Valley," and of Wes, like Milton's unfallen Adam, "in the yard pulling weeds." This odd little whiff of the pastoral emerges more fully and vividly in "Feathers," *Cathedral*'s opening act, where we see "pastures, rail fences, milk cows moving slowly toward old barns," along with "red-winged blackbirds on . . . fences, and pigeons circling around haylofts," and "gardens and such, wildflowers in bloom, and little houses set back from the road." As readerly devotees of Carver's circumscribed world, such moments tend to knock us out of our chairs (even if the idyllic potential here is tempered somewhat by "houses" and "fences," walled human shelters, markers which fence out and enclose); taking us away from the couch and kitchen and bedroom, allowing us gusts of fresh air, such glimpses make the dire outcomes of the stories even harder to take. Like Fran and her husband in "Feathers," near newlyweds on the road to unhappiness, Edna and Wes (along with the reader) get a taste of the good life, of sweet living, as if only to heighten the sense of the bitter life they end up with.

Endless summers do indeed end, as "Chef's House" suggests, and security, along with the temporary comfort security tends to provide, is far from unassailable. From the beginning in Carver one's havens are subject to onslaught from without, be they onslaughts by ex-lovers, door-to-door salesmen, wrong number callers — even a cat can unnerve, a dead mouse at its feet, gazing ominously in from the hall. Disorder reigns in Carver's unstable universe, from the least to most positive story. Thus when Chef returns to reclaim what is his — the story's title, in its subtle, after-the-fact way, drives the point home — he returns as the invader, an inevitable force from without, however benevolent he may actually be. (Chef is a "recovered alcoholic," appropriately enough — if there is such a thing — unlike Wes, who is recovering, precariously riding his "wagon.") If the house stands as Wes's good luck charm, a talisman to help him effect a magical cure, then the sudden loss of the house stands to say that such cures are impossible, that good luck and magic do not exist.

"The story moves along on its own plateau of inexorability," Irving Howe writes. "It seems to whisper: There is a limit to what we can bear and sometimes a trivial event can crush us."[6] Undone by this turn in his life, crushed by unlucky circumstance and the prospect of uninsulated living, sickened by the thought of Fat Linda, Chef's daughter (evidently a drinker, somebody Wes knows from "his drinking days") taking over his sanctuary, Wes can't "suppose," as his wife bids him to do, that "this was for the first time," that "none of the other ever happened." He can "imagine no such power and freedom for himself," to use Eugene Goodheart's phrase, because thanks to his past he is no longer equipped with that kind of imagination.[7] The recovery-in-progress is over, in Wes's mind, as is his semi-revivified marriage (both he and his wife, reflecting on the summer they had, adopt the past tense in the end). Forecasting more serious drinking to come, Wes "picks up his cup and taste[s] from it" — the fruit juice, it seems, is not now as sweet as it was. Contrary to what he said at the outset, there is no starting over; for Wes and for others, Eden is a place one knows only once, if at all. Still clinging to his ruptured security, the protective walls that now fail to protect, he momentarily closes his eyes, sealing himself up in himself. Then he stands and, adding insult to injury, closes the drapes in broad daylight.

"[J]ust like that," Edna says, conveying her sense of the abruptness of things, the sea disappears. Early in the story, looming right outside the "front window," the ocean lent itself to the idyllic setting, to the sense of a low-rent couple with a millionaire's view, transported to paradise. In the story's last sentences, however, the sea is both a sorry reminder of what Wes has lost and a vast, impersonal thing, both the killer and burial place of Fat Linda's husband, perhaps — Wes will himself be drowning soon, we can't help but think, in his own kind of liquid — and an emblem of the chaos that governs him. (The northern California coast is notoriously dangerous, incidentally, especially in summer, when "sneaker waves" sweep people away; it is no accident that Wes and Linda fish in "lagoons.") Pulling the curtains, Wes shuts out chaos and Eden in a simultaneous gesture, and at the same time locks himself and Edna in with despair, with the sudden shipwreck of his dreams.

What makes "Chef's House" different from its predecessors — dark as it is, beyond those small glints of the pastoral — is that Edna and Wes actually communicate, even when Wes, like many silent figures before him, fails to speak. They are surprisingly in touch with each other, despite the little good that it does them. Watching as he visibly crumbles, Edna tunes in to her husband, explaining that he doesn't "say anything else," that he doesn't "have to." She sees him "touching his lips with his tongue" and "thumbing his shirt under his waistband," and, reading the nonverbal signs, concludes that once the few fish in the "icebox" are gone (another enclosure, looking forward to "Boxes," one of Carver's last stories), once their last supper is over, "that will be the end of it." Wes, too, is terribly aware, fatalist that he is. Unlike James Packer in "After the Denim," enraged, furiously stabbing cloth with a needle, Wes is a thinker ("he *was* thinking," Edna says) and a decision-maker ("He seemed to have made up his mind.") Like Fran's husband in "Feathers," reminiscing about a shining night in his newlywed life, Wes has a clear sense of what he has lost. Putting his understanding to work, he collaborates in his own undoing; he makes up his mind. His decision makes the name of the town where the story is located especially ironic — "Eureka," evoking both discovery and taking possession. What Wes discovers is that possession in all forms is illusory, and that what we do take we often find taken away.

In this sense Wes is hardly unique. "The characters in the later stories," Carver says in an interview, "are not destitute or trapped or beaten up by circumstances. It's a life they may have asked for once, but simply don't want any longer. They make decisions."[8] Frail as he is, though stronger than Carver's earlier figures, Wes is empowered by choice. Existentially humanist in its orientation, "Chef's House," as a transitional story, signals a growing awareness on the parts of Carver's late figures, even if in this case awareness means only a sense of one's own doomed condition, and a willing compliance with that unavoidable doom, once one's peacocks begin to fade from the picture. As in much of *Cathedral*, we find freedom residing within oppressive constraint, even if this bleak freedom means little more than the freedom to pull the curtains on hope, or pull down our already-falling-down walls; even if freedom lies in the knowledge, as Carver's survivors tend to discover, that all our houses are borrowed, whether we own them or not.

In "Where I'm Calling From" we find another man trying to come to grips with alcoholism, this time within the enclosed environment of an alcohol treatment home. Unlike Meyers in his compartment, or Lloyd in his garrett, or Sandy's husband in his insular living room — men self-barricaded in ways as offensive to others as they are destructive to self — this speaker's confinement, like Wes's, is both positive and necessary. Until lately he has insulated himself with the buffering torpor booze provides, his addiction both a reaction to and the cause of his failing marriage; now he locks himself up voluntarily in "Frank Martin's drying out facility." Arriving at Frank Martin's dead drunk (but a stronger version of Wes in the end), he exchanges one state of insularity for another, taking refuge from his prior refuge, the one that was killing him. Sitting on the porch with another recovering drunk, J. P., he takes further comfort in the story his new friend has to tell.[9]

It is significant that throughout most of the story Carver leaves his characters sitting where they are. Protected yet still exposed to the chill of the outer world, the porch is a liminal space existing between the internal security of the cure-in-progress and the lure, and danger, of the outer world. On the porch, the narrator and J. P. are at once sheltered and vulnerable, their immediate physical surroundings an objective correlative to the transitional state of their minds and wills. Beyond the "green hill" they see from the porch, as Frank Martin tells them, is Jack London's house, the place where the famous author lived until "alcohol killed him." Beyond that — much farther north — is the "Yukon," the fictive topos of London's "To Build a Fire," a place where, as the narrator recalls later, a man will "actually . . . freeze to death if he can't get a fire going." With his wet clothes London's figure is hardly well-insulated, even though, ironically, he's bundled up in the manner of Carver's story's two strongest figures: J. P.'s wife, Roxy (whose "big knuckles" have broken her husband's nose) wears both a "coat" and "a heavy sweater"; Frank Martin, hard-edged and tough and looking like a "prizefighter," keeps his "sweater buttoned all the way up."

Sitting alone, enjoying the transitional comforts of the porch, Carver's speaker fails to recall, or subconsciously omits, the sad conclusion of London's tale — that, at the mercy of the elements, London's man eventually freezes, his life extinguished along with his fire. Still upset about Tiny's "seizure," it seems, he chooses not to think of the extreme consequences of ill-prepared exposure to the outer world, nor does he remind himself that death had entered the heart of the sanctuary only days before, this time without claiming its prize. Subject also to bodily complaints, J. P. suffers from the "shakes" and the narrator from an occasional "jerk in [his] shoulder"; like Tiny, the fat electrician from Santa Rosa, J. P. and his friend are each in their own way overpowered by biology, by nature. Their bodies adjust and compensate as they recover, as do their minds. And just as love was once "something that was out of [J. P.'s] hands" — a thing which set his "legs atremble" and filled him "with sensations that were carrying him every which way" — the aftermath of drinking is for the narrator superseded in intensity only by death, the ultimate spasm, a force proceeding from within as well as from without, over which insulation has no power at all.

Before "going inside," Frank recommends a bit of reading, namely *The Call of the Wild*; "We have it inside if you want to read something," he tells J. P. and the speaker. "It's about this animal that's half dog and half wolf." The narrator is similarly divided, torn by inner impulses. At the outset of his first visit, Frank had taken him aside, saying, "We can help you. If you want help and want to listen to what we say"; thinking now in retrospect, he admits, "I didn't know if they could help me or not. Part of me wanted help. But there was another part." Partly civilized, partly wild, he is in a very real way protecting himself from himself. His retreat at Frank Martin's is an attempt at self-domestication that, considering his present predicament, has failed him before. Caught up in a veritable war of selves, blown by the aftermath of addiction, literally vibrating in his chair, he is "not out of the woods yet," as he tells J. P. "In-between women," Skenazy writes, "in-between homes, in-between drinks, the narrator locates himself in his disintegration."[10] In this in-between world he begins to come to terms with disintegration, and begins imagining ways to reintegrate and rebuild.

Above all he wants "to listen," as Frank Martin says, though it is not Frank he chiefly listens to but J. P. "Keep talking, J. P.," he says early on.

"You better keep talking," he says, interjecting this and like phrases throughout the story in the manner of a refrain. Emergence from hardened insularity is connected to listening, to intensive listening. It is as necessary for him as *telling* is for J. P. and for Carlyle in "Fever," who emerges from a psychological and physical ordeal by unloading his pent-up turmoils verbally on his babysitter. In "Where I'm Calling From," the process of coming out involves *moving into* the narrative of another, entering imaginatively into a discourse which, arising of the communal act of storytelling, is at once familiar and unfamiliar. Since "commiseration instigates recuperation," as Arthur Saltzman observes of this tale, J. P. 's story initiates by means of both fellowship and displacement the continuation of the narrator's own story — and, if he is lucky, the reassembly of his fragmented life.[11] But there are perils as well as benefits in such transactions, in sharing stories. In "Will You Please Be Quiet, Please," a secure, relatively happy man becomes distraught at hearing the tale of his wife's infidelity, a tale she tells him herself. Rudy's recollection of his overweight classmates in "Fat," a misfired attempt at warm conversation, embitters his bitter wife all the more. In "Sacks," a son self-enclosed by concerns meets his father briefly in an airport, and hearing the story of his father's adultery, cuts himself off from his father for good, utterly alienated by the old man's confession.

Before *Cathedral*, extended verbal transaction — if transaction takes place at all — usually constitutes perilous intercourse indeed. In "Where I'm Calling From," however, as in other stories of this volume, Carver would have us believe otherwise. "I'm listening," the speaker says, waiting for J. P. to go on with his tale. "It's helping me to relax, for one thing. It's taking me away from my own situation." J. P. 's story helps him do more than merely "relax." Listening, and the imagination required for close listening, takes him away from his "own situation" even as it brings him closer to the heart of his problems. His inner crisis is externalized in J. P. 's story, both in the pairing of their present circumstances and in the details of his friend's narration — in such odd details, in fact, as the "well" J. P. fell into as a boy. Like the chimneys from which J. P. makes his livelihood later in life (narrow, tubular enclosures associated with the family to whom he becomes attached — they run a chimney-sweep business), the well is a trap, a darkly insulating prison; it represents the extent to which J. P. senses, enclosed until very recently in a bottle, he has hit "bottom" in the present trajectory of his life.[12] For the narrator and J. P. alike, the well represents the pitfalls of experience, the dark places they have found themselves in, places they are extricated from ultimately only through the intervening efforts of others. Like J. P. "hollering" at the bottom of the well, the narrator waits for a dropline of his own, his "line out" being (along with his willingness to reform) the telephone. By the end of the story he has tried calling his wife twice and is about to call his "girlfriend," hoping to reestablish contact with the women in his life, not to mention with the outer world — hence the story's title. Not by any means out of the woods yet, though, he still wavers in his resolve. In one of the story's last lines, thinking of his girlfriend, he says, "Maybe I'll call her first" — suggesting, given what we know about her drinking, that this line out may send him tumbling back into the hole. Torn between the warmth of stability and the chill of the outer world, between civilization and wilderness, he continues his war with himself.

Mildly obsessed with the women in his life, he has two layers of female protection, in a sense buffering him from the world. It is not surprising, then, that his life and J. P.'s story intersect finally in a woman's kiss. Rather more hopeful than the peacock in "Feathers" — one man's radiant token of bliss he'll never know — Roxy's kiss is a token of "luck" emphasizing more than this speaker's need for help from without, for a rope down the well of his life. As a gesture, Roxy's kiss underscores the degree to which women provide him much-needed security; he has in the past depended on women, perhaps, as much as he has on drink, or does now on the captivating flow of J. P.'s narrative. Our sense of this man's greatest personal security, in fact, comes with a recollection of his wife and him in the bedroom — that morning, long ago, when the landlord came around to paint the house:

I push the curtain away from the window. Outside, this old guy in white coveralls is standing next to his ladder. The sun is just starting to break over the mountains. The old guy and I look each other over. It's the landlord, all right — this old guy in coveralls. But his coveralls are too big for him. He needs a shave, too. And he's wearing this baseball cap to cover his bald head. Goddamn it, I think, if he isn't a weird old fellow. And a wave of happiness comes over me that I'm not him — that I'm me and that I'm inside this bedroom with my wife. (145)

Seated on "the front steps" in the chill air beyond the porch, the narrator warms himself with this memory of the past, a memory seemingly triggered by the kiss he gets from Roxy (before she and J. P. "go in," leaving him outside alone). He associates his past "happiness," then, with being "inside" with his wife in the bedroom, suggesting not only how much women are integral to his well-being but also how beneficial certain walls and enclosures have been to him at various times. "Outside," as in the form of a strange, skinny old man, are reminders of toil and old age, and, as before, of what lies beyond that — illness and decrepitude and death. "[I]nside," on the contrary, there is security and leisure, embodied by a laughing wife, the enveloping comforts of a warm bed, and the recognition of his circumstances as being as secure as they then were.

Thus the contact the narrator makes with an old man one morning is recapitulated by his contact with a younger man years later, though contact is closer now since both men are "outside," and working together to find ways back in. Epitomized in the gesture of Roxy's kiss, the intersecting of their lives and stories initiates a recuperation that may or may not get them, as J. P. says, "back on the track." With disruptions in time and in narrative continuity that mirror the psychic state of the narrator, the story wanders from man to man in its focus, intertwining the individual threads of their stories, rendering them oddly inseparable, fusing them in the brotherly knit of the text. By promoting such healthy complicity, such intersections, "Where I'm Calling From" embodies and dramatizes our tendency to discover ourselves in the stories of others, to complicate other lives with our own as we collaborate toward understanding, toward liberation from the confinements that kill.

"A Small, Good Thing" presents a similar intersecting of lives, more disparate, but with problems no less vivid and serious. It is the story of a couple dealing with the loss of a child, and of the consolation they find eventually, haphazardly, in the company of a baker; it is a story about grief and worry and fear, and about how disaster can crack one's insulating though eggshell-thin sense of habitual security. It is also, like "The Third Thing" and other stories, about how the narratives of others can cushion the violent unsettling such cracking brings on. As in "Where I'm Calling From," recovery is connected to listening, to opening oneself to others through channels of verbal interaction. In this story, however —

perhaps because its central figures, Ann and Howard Weiss, are simultaneously more stable and more emotionally vulnerable than J. P. and his friend, and because the story evokes a greater sense of affirmation in general — the liberating aspects of attentive listening are more noticeable. With a fullness and optimism unequalled in any other story, Carver dramatizes here what William Stull calls "talk that works." [13] He provides here an answer to the failures his characters have been subject to all along, failures of characters in all of his books, who talk and listen with characteristically poor results. [14]

Corresponding to this new fullness of possibility, the story itself swells to new proportions (revised from its original form as "The Bath"), reflecting aesthetically and spatially the kind of psychological and spiritual expansion taking place within, on the level of theme. As Kathleen Shute writes of the revised story, "Carver not only confronts death here — a victory in itself — but goes on to record the life after, the agony and resulting growth of those who survive." [15] Thus "what began in 'The Bath' as an existential chronicle of Hopelessville," Stull writes, "becomes in 'A Small, Good Thing' a rich demonstration of what George Eliot called 'the secret of deep human sympathy.'" [16]

"So far," we hear of Howard Weiss, "he had kept away from any real harm, from those forces he knew existed and that could cripple or bring down a man if the luck went bad, if things suddenly turned." As it is for J. P.'s friend, "luck" is of crucial importance to Howard; its capriciousness, he understands, dictates over the details of his world — has in fact allowed "forces" to insinuate themselves into the placid interior of his life, forces manifesting themselves, after the initial blow in the form of a car, in the ominous calls of the baker. Howard's insular bubble of security on the point of bursting, he remains sealed in his "car for a minute" in the driveway, his leg beginning to "tremble" as he considers the gravity of his circumstances. Trying to "deal with the present situation in a rational manner," his motor control is almost as erratic as that of Frank Martin's clients. Similarly affected, Ann's teeth begin to "chatter" as fear begins to take over, as she realizes that she and her husband are "into something now, something hard." Like recovering alcoholics, both are afflicted by an irrational power in the face of which rationality is useless. The walls of their once-secure and self-enclosed familial world have, thanks to a bit of bad luck, crumbled with alarming speed, such that Weiss's lives are literally shaken by circumstance.

As the focal figure of the story, Ann comes across as both more preoccupied and more sensitive than her husband, not necessarily because her parental (maternal) attachment to the boy is greater than Howard's, but because she is afforded more interior space throughout the story. Despite the intensity of her preoccupation in their days-long vigil, therefore, she momentarily glimpses new walls around her, walls self-erected in the tide of catastrophe. "For the first time," the narrator says, describing Ann's realization after many hours in the hospital, "she felt they were together in it, this trouble." Realizing she has shut herself off to everything but her son and his condition, she acknowledges "She hadn't let Howard into it, though he was there and needed all along. She felt glad to be his wife." If the disruptive force of calamity clarifies, it also causes both Ann and her husband, hemmed in now by fear and dread, to project outward as they seek respite from confinement. Worry insulating them as security had before, they stand staring "out at the parking lot." They don't "say anything. But they seem . . . to feel each other's insides now, as though the worry had made them transparent in a perfectly natural way." Their interior state of affairs is "natural," of course, because it is *nature*, and their powerlessness in the face of it, that makes them transparent, that prompts them, fire-distilled now by mutual concern, to gaze out the window in a way that recalls J. P. and his friend on the porch. "This spiritual transparency," Stull notes, "makes a stark contrast to the existential opacity of the original characters" in "The Bath."[17] The "ability of one character to empathize with another's inarticulation," Michael Gearhart writes of this story, "is a rarity in Carver's fiction" — and a phenomenon, we might add, unprecedented in Carver's work until this story.[18]

The verbal connections taking place in the story, are unprecedented as well. As in "Where I'm Calling From," the act of exchanging stories serves as a refuge, though here an even more compensatory one. Ann and Howard end up in a bakery, giving up the oppressive environment of the hospital and a house full of painful momentoes for a warmer, more spacious setting. The verbal transaction in the bakery is for both husband and wife (to use the doctor's mistaken diagnosis regarding Scotty's "deep sleep") a kind of "restorative measure"; at the hands of the baker the

Weisses are doctored as their son could not be. Unlike J. P. and his friend, however, they are consoled by a man who cannot truly identify or empathize, a man as ironically unlike them as anybody could be. "I don't have any children myself," the baker tells Howard and Ann, "so I can only imagine what you must be feeling." Still, sparked by his power to "imagine" their grief, he begins his tale of "loneliness, and of . . . what it was like to be childless all these years," offering them if nothing else at least the consolation of knowing that they know what they are going to miss. Thus husband and wife listen, and listening, enter the baker's world — his story — to temporarily escape their own. "They listened carefully," the narrator says, drawing special attention to the act through repetition: "they listened to what the baker had to say."

Elsewhere in *Cathedral*, hearing and listening are treated in less optimistic terms. In "Careful," Lloyd's metaphorical deafness to the world is figured in the literal blockage of his ear with wax. In "Vitamins," a similar if more general deafness finds its emblem in the form of a dismembered, dried-out human ear. But in other stories — in "Fever" and "Where I'm Calling From," for instance — characters indeed turn their ears to others, and come away better for it. "I got ears," blind Robert says in "Cathedral," affirming, in spite of his handicap, that "Learning never ends." "Intimacy," one of Carver's last stories, features a fiction writing narrator who calls himself "all ears," at once a plunderer of experience (like his predecessor in "Put Yourself in My Shoes") and a meticulous listener, a person who by way of listening carefully reconstructs memory to reorder the disorder of his past. In "A Small, Good Thing," more strikingly than ever, telling and listening are beneficial, recuperative activities. What is crucial here is not so much the substance of the stories characters tell as the process of telling. ("I was interested," J. P.'s friend says of J. P.'s tale; "But I would have listened if he'd been going on about how one day he'd decided to start pitching horseshoes.") Enveloped in the baker's tale, Ann and Howard listen and listen, escaping the still unthinkable reality of their present circumstances by entering the stifling, insulated, private life of their host, thus beginning their slow journey out of the darkness of grief. Though it is still dark outside, it is "like daylight" inside the bakery. Warmed by the light and the ovens and the sweet rolls they eat, revived by mutual compassion, Ann and Howard do "not think of leaving."

From the shadowy, overdetermined world of "The Bath," then, where the tiny enclosure of a bathtub provides a sole comfort for characters ("Fear made him want to take a bath," the original narrator says of Howard), we traverse to the indoor daylight of the bakery, where food and talk and commiseration actually do make a difference, if not redeeming characters of their misery at least affording them comfort, allowing them to see that loneliness and hardship and death are part of the natural order of things and that as people they can share their aloneness. The welcome light of possibility and potential self-regeneration is also reflected in the overall shape of the story; "A Small, Good Thing" is two-thirds again as long as the original story and the longest story Carver ever published. "I went back to that one," he said in an interview,

as well as several others, because I felt there was unfinished business that needed attending to. The story hadn't been told originally; it had been messed around with, condensed and compressed in "The Bath" to highlight the qualities of menace that I wanted to emphasize . . . so in the midst of writing these other stories for Cathedral I went back to "The Bath" and tried to see what aspects of it needed to be enhanced, redrawn, reimagined.[19]

Enhanced and redrawn, the story is nevertheless still in many ways characteristic of Carver. The "one in a million circumstance" of Scotty's "hidden occlusion," as Kathleen Shute observes, demonstrates that "even in this more optimistic universe, a blind and inexplicable randomness still lurks, shaping and destroying at will."[20] Thus "even as [Carver] makes the characters more sympathetic," Stull notes, "he remains true to the harsh existential premises of the story."[21] Carver remains true to himself, in other words, altering his artistic methods but preserving the core of his vision as he moves from contraction to expansion. Comparing its spareness to the fullness of Cathedral, Carver says of What We Talk About When We Talk About Love, "Everything I thought I could live without I just got rid of, I cut out . . . It felt like I'd gone as far in that direction as I wished to go."[22] Radically changing direction, reexploring old subjects while delving into unfinished business, Carver illustrates in this writerly expansion how fully an artist can break down the self-fashioned walls of style and still maintain his signature. Not unlike a few of his more fortunate characters, Carver exhanges an enclosing environment for greater capaciousness, for a new but not unfamiliar direction, and, we tend to suppose, for a new sense of himself.

More frequently anthologized than any other story by Carver, "Cathedral" charts the coming out of a self-insulated figure more dramatically than ever before, a man who, unlike Myers running from the world on a train bound for nowhere, begins to sense the seriousness of his insularity. Hemmed in by insecurity and prejudice, buffered by drink and pot and by the sad fact, as his wife says, that he has no "friends," he is badly out of touch with his world, his wife, and himself. But as in "A Small, Good Thing" and "Where I'm Calling From," and less optimistically in "Chef's House," he emerges from enclosure and transcends his self-strictures, although this story affords neither release nor any semi-conscious decision, but rather a nonverbal act — an odd, unspoken transaction taking place between him and his blind guest. As is often the case with Carver's characters, talk fails here, and yet this man's failure is more than made up for by the connection he succeeds in making at last, by the self-liberating results of his trial.

Recalling Howard and Ann Weiss, and Wes in his idyllic retreat, his narrow, sheltered world is abruptly threatened from without. The appearance of his wife's friend Robert constitutes, at least at the outset, an invasion of his hermetic existence. "A blind man in my house was not something I looked forward to," he says, and later adds, "Now this same blind man was coming to sleep in my house." His territorial impulses, spurred by insecurity and repulsion and fear, make for what Skenazy calls an "evening of polite antagonism between the two men." [23] His buried hostility, we are led to suppose, is rooted in part in Robert's association with his wife's past, a past that intimidates him — particularly her former marriage, a subject with which he is obsessed. Simultaneously fascinated by and reluctant to hear the blind man's story ("my wife filled me in with more details than I cared to know," he says; "I made a drink and sat at the kitchen table to listen") he at least indirectly seeks, in his wife's dealings with Robert, some sense of himself, of self-image. Like J. P.'s friend, this man's identity is connected to his bond with a female, a bond he needs to see perpetually reinforced — although, justly perturbed by his insensitivity, his wife does not give him the reinforcement he craves. Referring to his wife's conversation with Robert in the living room, he says, "I waited

in vain to hear my name on my wife's sweet lips." His muddled search
for self involves a continual gauging and protecting of the autocratic status of his name. A year earlier, hearing a taped conversation between his
wife and her friend, he'd been startled to hear his "own name in the
mouth of [a] stranger, this blind man." Determined to assert himself, ineffective as his methods may seem, he blankets his wife's past the way he
has lately blanketed his present — with insulating self-absorbency. Sum-
ming up his wife's prior life, he calls her ex-husband her "officer," adding, "Why should he have a name?" No ideal listener, and short on compassion, he predicates the names and stories of others under the heading
of his own tyrannical if precarious identity, listening for purposes of self-
validation, relegating the rest of experience, including Robert's marriage,
to a place "beyond [his] understanding."

It is fitting that Robert, the invader in the house, is insulated only
physically, left in the dark only by his handicap. Extremely outgoing and
friendly, he has done "a little of everything," from running a sales dis-
tributorship to traveling in Mexico to broadcasting "ham radio." His activities, unlike those of his host, take him out into the world, his boom-
ing voice having extended as far as "Alaska" and "Tahiti" on the airwaves
before making its way into the narrator's home. Unlike the baker and
J. P. — restrained men in comparison — Robert is pure blazing personal-
ity, an extradurable and appropriate guide, a man capable of pulling his
host from his shell. (Like the Weisses, however, Robert also is grieving,
having just lost his wife; "I know about skeletons," he says, regarding the
show on TV). As Robert's host fails to describe what he sees on the television, Robert listens, and having "listened" to failure, takes charge of the
situation. "Hey, listen to me," he says, activated suddenly by his host's admission of verbal defeat. "Will you do me a favor? I got an idea. Why
don't you find us some heavy paper. And a pen. We'll do something. We'll
draw one together. Get us a pen and some heavy paper. Go on, bub, get
the stuff." Robert's initiative here, and the remedy he momentarily employs, suggests that verbal handicaps — not to mention the larger problems of which they are symptoms — are like unto blindness, debilitations
stemming from the willed blindness of oversight, of poor insight, of ig-
norance. The way Robert takes charge and plays the role of the teacher
(his gray beard implying, on some quiet level, wisdom) suggests that

handicaps are first and foremost challenges, hurdles we surmount and pass over.

Regarding the joint project of the drawing, Michael Vander Weele writes, "most of the communication in this story comes through shared non-verbal work, as expression that stops short of the effort and commonality of speech."[24] A true case of the blind leading the blind, drawing the cathedral is a "gesture of fraternity," as Howe observes, which, like the meal preceding it, promotes human contact and finally nudges the narrator, if only temporarily, out of his self-contained world.[25] The subject and product of their mutual efforts, the cathedral — like all of Carver's symbols — represents mainly itself, an old thing made of stone, though its metaphorical resonances (concerning common humanity, benevolence and good will, patient human effort and fortitude in the act of "a-spiring") are palpable, if typically non-insistent, in the story.[26] Curiously, the speaker ultimately ends up within the walls of his own handmade cathedral. "I was in my house," he says when he finishes, eyes still tightly closed, bringing to mind the "box" he drew when he and Robert began, a figure that "could have been the house [he] lived in." What begins, therefore, as the enclosing spatial configuration of his home — and of his present level of awareness, we guess — gradually swells in proportion to become something more spacious, something awesome and utterly new, its interior depths as enlightening to him as bakeries and bedrooms are comforting to others.

"As in D. H. Lawrence's story 'The Blind Man,'" Goodheart observes, "blindness becomes a metaphor for imagination: the power of the mind to ascend to the spires."[27] "I didn't feel like I was inside anything," the narrator says, still unwilling to open his eyes, in a sense blinding himself in order to see. While Myers "close[s] his eyes" to whatever encroaches on his personal life (his voluntary blindness as bad as Lloyd's deafness), this man finds not escape or evasion but finally discovery in self-enclosure, a discovery made possible by his willingness to delve into that inner vestibule of self, where selfishness gives way at last to self-awareness. A man obsessed with the faculty of vision ("Imagine," he says of Robert's wife early on, "a woman who could never see herself as she was seen in the eyes of her loved one"), he clings now to a miraculous glimpse of a world beyond insular life, remaining willingly blind to the distracting reality of his former world, even as Robert calls him back. "It was like nothing else in my life up to now," he says, staggered by new awareness, adding, in the story's final sentence, "It's really something." The indefiniteness of his language — he is usually more glib than he seems here — expresses both the sheer incomprehensibility of his revelation and the fact that he registers it as such. He falls into "depths of feeling that he need not name to justify," as one critic writes, feelings of an intensity unmatched anywhere else in Carver's fiction.[28]

Transcendence, of course, has lurked in Carver's work since the earliest stories, evidenced by the "impossible changes" Ralph Wyman undergoes in "Will You Please Be Quiet, Please?" where jealousy and self-preoccupation are neutralized in the end by human contact, by something much larger than words. Just as Ann Weiss wants "her words to be her own" after the death of her son, shopping for a private vocabulary of grief, the man in "Cathedral" gropes for words weighty enough to fit his experience, and failing gloriously in that, settles for indefinites. Impossibly changed, reduced to semi-inarticulateness, he keeps his eyes fastened shut, wavering between awareness and habitual existence, there in his new and newly spacious enclosure. He is "no longer inside himself," as Skenazy writes, "if not quite outside, no longer alone, if not quite intimate."[29]

The tonal shift in the final sequence of the story, then, marked by the mild ethereality flooding the last lines, itself illustrates the opening up the narrator has undergone, and is yet to undergo. Like Robert, on a journey by train, dropping in on friends and relatives, trying to get over the loss of his wife, the narrator is also on a journey, one signaled by signposts in his language and played out by the events of the story he tells. (Early in the story, he feels momentarily "sorry for the blind man," his insulated hardness beginning to soften; as the walls of his resentment noticeably crack, he watches with "admiration" as Robert eats, recognizing that Robert's handicap is no impairment to his performance at the dinner table.) This man's destination, like that of all Carver's travelers — whether they leave home or not — is necessarily a confining one. But it is also a destination where one's sense of shared confinement makes for heretofore unknown freedoms. "What's a cathedral without people?" Robert asks, bidding his host to add a touch of humanity to the drawing, to "put

some people in there." Approaching his new destination, the narrator begins to realize just how exhilarating confinement can be, once one sees
beyond the narrow enclosure of self that larger, more expansive enclosure
of society. The warmth of the blind man's touch still alive in his hand, he
begins to sense — as did perhaps the builders who toiled for years to
raise cathedrals they would never see, people who were, as Robert says,
"no different than the rest of us" — that we're all in this together, and
that that really *is* something.

Carver wrote "Cathedral" on a train, during a transcontinental journey from Seattle to New York.[30] Enclosed in tight quarters, rubbing
shoulders with people, going somewhere in a hurry: the writing environment seems an appropriate one, considering the nature of the story,
and of the book of stories, which was to come of that ride. "I knew that
story was different from anything I'd ever written," Carver told an inter-
viewer, explaining that "Cathedral" was first in the batch, "and all of the
stories after that seemed to be fuller somehow and much more generous
and maybe more affirmative."[31] The flashpoint of a self-revising, self-ex-
panding fire, the story witnesses "an effort on Carver's part to transcend
his medium," as one critic observes. Or, as Carver says in a preface to
*Where I'm Calling From,* "Somehow I had found another direction I
wanted to move toward. And I moved. And quickly."[32] In *Cathedral* Carver
has traversed a great distance; as in no other volume, characters *connect*
with one another and, however briefly, come away changed. Still, such
momentary connections do not reflect the tone of the book as a whole.
Most stories — "The Compartment," say, or "The Train," ironically stories
about people on trains or in train stations — are slightly fuller explora-
tions of Carver's old familiar territory, reimmersions into tableaux where
human proximity only heightens disconnectedness, where alienation
comes hand-in-hand with self-insulation. It is important to note that
Carver describes the stories as only "maybe" more affirmative, unwilling
to see only light in his primarily dark world. Explaining his new optimism in terms of the events of his life, he says

*I believe now that the world will exist for me tomorrow in the same way it exists
for me today. That didn't used to be the case. For a long time I found myself living
by the seat of my pants, making things terribly difficult for myself and  everyone
around me by my drinking. In this second life, this post-drinking life, I still re-*

tain a certain sense of pessimism, I suppose, but I also have belief in and love for the things of this world. [33]

Brightened by his "second life" but forever tapping into the first, Carver hands us pessimism and optimism in the same package — hands us Wes, sealed up inside Chef's house in the dark with new knowledge of doom, and hands us Holits, in "The Bridle," whose metaphorical freedom takes the form of a swan dive from atop a cabana, a dive Holits miscalculates, missing the pool to crack his head on the concrete. In general, however, in both darkness and light, Carver suggests that life hemmed in by walls is a hard life indeed. Contrary to Myers's reflection that being fully walled in might be "a good way to live," we suspect just the opposite, deploring with Carver this business of having a ticket but no idea where one is riding, and no connection with one's fellow travelers.

It is through our collaboration with others, Carver implies, that we free ourselves from the slavery of self-absorption. We see in *Cathedral* that compassion is a prerequisite not just of happiness but of survival; we see that while confinement may be a precondition of many lives, freedom still exists within such confinement, freedom which becomes tangible only when recognized for what it is. In this sense, these stories are similar to those Carver and Jenks praise as editors of *American Short Story Masterpieces*, stories which have, as they say, "the ambition of enlarging our view of ourselves and the world." [34] Enlarging us as readers, that is, both expanding us and setting us free.

# Chapter Four

"THINGS CLEARLY WITHIN MY POWER": COMMUNICATION AND CONTROL IN THE LAST STORIES

"What can I but enumerate old themes?" W. B. Yeats asks in a poem, inventorying the figures and topics recurring in his work over the years. Heading likewise toward the place where, as Yeats writes, "all the ladders start" Carver returns in his final published work to the old "obsessions," reexploring the subjects closest to both his heart and the heart of his aesthetic enterprise. As Tess Gallagher notes in her introduction to *A New Path to the Waterfall*, "There was an urge in Ray's [later] writing, in both the poems and stories, to revisit certain evocative scenes and characters in his life, to wrest from them if not release, then at least a telling anatomy of the occasion."[1] Collected as "New Stories" in *Where I'm Calling From*, the last seven stories indeed provide an illuminating anatomical look at Carver's preoccupations as a storyteller: in them we see the old familiar problems of marital and familial disharmony; we see dramatized again that strain of agonized suburban alienation. Most striking, we find an array of characters who struggle, mainly unsuccessfully, to comprehend the bleak realities of their lives. "What lasts is what you start with," to use Charles Wright's phrase, one Carver employs, fittingly, as an epigraph in *A New Path*, his final volume of poems.[2]

Despite all this, however, and despite a terminal illness, Carver did not choose to lay his ladder aside. The "New Stories" attest that he had many more rungs to climb, and that he climbed them. A number of the stories, for instance, deal in a surprisingly direct way with the subjects of reading and writing, addressed with an explicitness unprecedented in earlier books. Other stories confront death and mortality head-on, a subject present in Carver's work from the beginning, as one critic points out, but which emerges concretely only in the later work.[3] Combining new and old obsessions alike, the last stories extend and sharpen Carver's vision of human relationships even as they delimit the affimative potential of that vision, tempering to a degree the burgeoning optimism marking his preceding volume. The momentary optimism of *Cathedral*, in other words, does not exactly herald celebratory writings to come; instead, the last stories explore the "nature of captivity," as Arthur Saltzman notes, charting in new ways the range of individual mobility within what has in Carver been since the beginning an immobilizing, darkly circumscribed world.[4]

"I feel I don't have a choice in the matter any longer," one of Carver's late figures complains, describing his own obsessive responses to the disorder of his life.[5] We are all captives in various ways, Carver suggests; what passes for stability and control in our lives now and then is purely illusion, if not self-delusion. Baffled and paralyzed in the aftermath of divorce, or, more recently, glancing furtively into the maw of death, Carver's characters demonstrate how much larger and more complex are the patterns dictating life than are their individual powers of comprehension. Captives though they are, however, they are not without capacities, as in *Cathedral*, for glimpsing the forces and patterns that dominate them. What they do glimpse now and then — even if in the form of a merely potential release from captivity — comes most often in the form of some untried, uncustomary strategy of language: for one character potential release resides in a single word; for another it lies in a nonverbal sign; for others it comes of the activity of nocturnal conversation; for others, the self-enriching acts of reading and writing. Unlike the early figures, in whose worlds inarticulateness and hopelessness go hand-in-hand, Carver's last characters not only recognize freedom but typically *articulate* their recognitions, even if only to vent dismay at how impossible such freedom seems in relation to their lives. Newly articulate, increasingly self-aware, they embody on Carver's part a simultaneous closing down and opening up of hopeful possibility. Their various insights and, necessarily, their defeats, map out the lighter, more affirmative contours of a world perpetually darkened by captivity and constraint.

Taken as a whole, the last seven stories are as daring as anything Carver had done before, if not more so. They are more comprehensive, fuller rhetorically and thematically, while at the same time lighter in tone than the earlier work. Marilynne Robinson describes the stories as "more rueful and humorous, written in more elegant prose and more elegiac than the earlier ones."[6] Skenazy calls them "autumnal tales," noting that they are longer than usual, "more stately in cadence," and that the "language of observation and the exchanges between people are more generous."[7] Rueful and generous in subject and manner alike, the first of the last stories, "Boxes," explores from the outset the issue of captivity, as the title indicates. Like many in Carver country, the narrator and his girlfriend are recovering from divorce (they were both previously married), and, to complicate things, the narrator is "worried sick" about his mother, who has made moving from residence to residence a way of life, and who at age seventy is still itinerant as ever. Unlike others before him, this speaker is acutely aware of the problems he faces, and seems willing (where others before have been unwilling, unable, or both) to do something about them. The fullness of his comprehension is poignantly mirrored by Carver's new fullness of prose.

Explaining his impatience about joining his mother for one more of her many goodbye meals, he says, "I don't see my options," revealing out loud what earlier characters reflected through speechlessness and inarticulate dismay: a clearly defined outline of the trap he is caught in. This man is torn between what he considers his duty to his mother as a son and his disillusionment about the model of stability she represents in his life. Tied to his obligations — captive, as it were — he tries to ameliorate things by speaking to her (no easy task, thanks to her eccentricities, her prevailing negativity). While his mother complains on the phone, saying she doesn't want to "see this place again except from [her] coffin," he watches out the window:

> I remember hanging on to the phone and watching a man high up on a pole doing something to a power line. Snow whirled around his head. As I watched, he leaned out from the pole, supported only by his safety belt. Suppose he falls, I thought. I didn't have any idea what I was going to say next. I had to say something. But I was filled with unworthy feelings, thoughts no son should admit to. (308)

Identifying himself with the man on the pole, he underlines his vulnerability, his sense of vertiginous emotional exposure as he deals with his mother, and does so in a manner which is both strikingly self-aware and brutally honest. He recognizes, even if after the fact, his "unworthy feelings" for what they are, though this hardly makes communicating any easier. And abortive communication, as elsewhere in Carver, is a major issue in "Boxes." The kernel of the story exists as "Mother," a poem published several years earlier; it, too, presents a phone conversation, but presents a different picture of communication:

She hears me out. Then informs
me she's leaving this goddamn place. Somehow. The only time
she wants to see it, or me again, is from her coffin.
Suddenly, I ask if she remembers the time Dad
was dead drunk and bobbed the tail of the Labrador pup.
I go on like this for a while, talking about
those days. She listens, waiting her turn.
It continues to snow. It snows and snows
as I hang on the phone. The trees and rooftops
are covered with it.[8]

Besides the conspicuous absence of the man on the pole, and the added reference to the father's drunkenness (underplayed in "Boxes," or submerged and utilized as a trump card in the final moments of the story), the crucial item in "Mother" is that substantial verbal links between mother and son do not exist. Both listen, waiting their turns to speak, but their exchange is finally as cold and dead as the snow that blankets everything outside.

In "Boxes," similarly, phone conversations — there are three, providing in part the story's structure — are largely ineffective. To make matters worse, the live interchanges between mother and son hardly come off better. Describing the final exchange of goodbyes, the son says, "I stand there wanting to say something else. But I don't know what. We keep looking at each other, trying to smile and reassure each other." Sadly, despite his self-acknowledged shortcomings, he craves reassurance — this is what differentiates "Boxes" from "Mother," as well as from nearly all the stories which precede it. "You're my mother," he says, seeking remedy.

"What can I do to help?" What he lacks in the way of verbal successes is ironically compensated for, if not in some perverse way corrected by, the nonverbal gesturing that goes on in the story. Besides the supportive "patting" he receives from his girlfriend, the level of physicality in the story is unusually high. "[W]e hug each other," he says after Jill comes out of the bathroom, upset by the prospect of another meal with Mom; meeting his mother at the back door as they arrive for dinner, he says, "She hugs Jill, and then she hugs me . . . We finish hugging and go inside." Jill and his mother, though not fond of one another, respond in like manner and "hug each other when they say hello or goodbye."

The crucial embrace in the final sentences of the story is enacted, not accidentally, by a pair of non-characters, a man and woman who are strangers to us (and, evidently, to the narrator himself). After the final phone call from his mother — during which time he has been "standing at the window," as usual — the son looks out to see his neighbor arrive home, watching as the man gets out of his car to be greeted by his wife:

*"What is it you see out there, honey?" Jill says. "Tell me."*

*What's there to tell? The people over there embrace for a minute, and then they go inside the house together. They leave the light burning. Then they remember, and it goes out.* (316)

The metaphorical effect here, with the closing of the door and the extinguishing of the light, is not new in Carver's canon. In "Neighbors," Bill and Arlene Miller are cut off suddenly from the voyeuristic lure of the neighbor's apartment, finding themselves literally shut out, with the door locked and the key inside. In "What We Talk About When We Talk About Love," a pair of couples exhaust themselves less by drinking than by their fruitless symposium on love, and as evening falls they end up paralyzed by inertia, sitting in silence, "not one of [them] moving, not even when the room [goes] dark."[9] Likewise in "Boxes," the speaker is figuratively shut out and in the dark, looking out from his window. He senses the intimacy he sees from afar to be something that, given the instability of his past, he will never genuinely know. "This is what we want," Jill says a moment earlier, trying to divert his attention to the curtains in her catalogue. The mild irony here — thanks to Carver's timing, his rhetorical and figural juxtapositioning — underlines the despair his characters feel, and sometimes acknowledge, recognizing that domestic tranquility is not a thing that comes easy, something you can choose and order by mail. Out of the darkness of encroaching despair, however, comes affirmative light, optimism in the form of potential. Still hoping, as he says early in the story, to "figure this thing out," the son fixes on a single word, and uttering it into the phone, recognizes in it a source of power:

> I don't know why, but it's then I recall the affectionate name my dad used sometimes when he was talking nice to my mother — those times, that is, when he wasn't drunk. It was a long time ago, and I was a kid, but always, hearing it, I felt better, less afraid, more hopeful about the future. "Dear," he'd say. He called her "dear" sometimes — a sweet name. "Dear," he'd say . . .
> The word issues from my lips before I can think what else I want to say to go along with it. "Dear." I say it again. I call her "dear." (316)

With incantatory repetition, the word arises in him as a password to a stability he feels himself to have been continually deprived of; its talismanic energy guides him toward some new, however nostalgic, vision of domestic felicity. Although he is locked out and left in the dark, as the story's concluding sentences attest, there is still compensation in knowing that despite hopeless circumstances (his mother's obsessiveness, his inability to make her see her actions as such), he still has one hedge against hopelessness: a small, good thing in the form of word. Ironically, however, the word is foreign to him. He does not know what else "to say to go along with it" given the context of his experience, and thus of his present vocabulary. Having chanced upon this token — or better, having rediscovered it — he may indeed use it to his benefit, though always consciously, awkwardly; it is part of a language he will undoubtedly never learn to speak.

Still, boxed in as he is by circumstance and obligation, and thanks in part to his obsession with windows, he nevertheless sees through the enclosing walls, even if insight comes ultimately in the form of a tease. Unlike characters of earlier volumes, who, as Irving Howe writes, "cannot understand the nature of their deprivation," this character comprehends what he lacks but not the necessary means for replenishing his deficit.[10] As a representative tale, "Boxes" reflects both in characterization and theme the tenuous quality of the last stories in general, reflecting at once an expansion and constriction of hopeful possibility. Striving for "fuller forms of expression," Saltzman observes, "Carver seldom casts a wider net, but he does seem increasingly willing to qualify the nature of captivity."[11] Embodying such new willingness on Carver's part, the captives inhabiting these stories recognize in varying degrees the cold facts of captivity, then strain against those enclosing surfaces, pushing harder and harder, even if only, as Carver's speaker tells us in "Boxes," to feel "better, less afraid, more hopeful about the future."

One of Carver's last poems, "Miracle," features a man battered by his wife. Wiping blood from his face, gaping down from the window of the jet in which he rides with his wife, he imagines

> People pushing
> up to a full table, grace being said,
> hands joined together under roofs so solid
> they will never blow off those houses — houses where,
> he imagines, decent people live and eat, pray
> and pull together. [12]

Familial and conjugal stability seems so utterly intangible to this poem's persona that it is recognizable only from a distance, through, as in "Boxes," the buffering insulation of glass and space. In another of the last stories, "Menudo," a character similarly gauges his domestic shortcomings by what he perceives to be the happy fulfillments of others. "I wish I could be like everybody else in this neighborhood," he says, bitter about the present chaos of his life, "your basic normal, unaccomplished person — and go up to my bedroom, and lie down, and sleep." Everywhere in Carver we see people holding yardsticks up to others, usually finding that they themselves don't measure up. In "Boxes" the neighbors provide the comparison; in "Menudo" it is the neighborhood. Not unlike Duane in "Gazebo," this story's speaker, Hughes, is paying for the consequences of adultery, unable to sleep in peace with his wife now that he has "forfeited that right." Cut off from "normal" happiness (not to mention hit "a few times in the head" by his wife), he says, "I'm outside all that now, and I can't get back inside!"

Much of the story consists of Hughes's insomnic musings and self-reproaches downstairs in his living room, in the dark. Like many of

Carver's later characters, he attempts to shore up his life — his ruined marriage, his discovered affair, his residual guilt regarding both an ex-wife (institutionalized in the wake of their divorce) and his mother (dead after a period of neglect on his part) — even as he admits his powerlessness in the face of the task. "I wish I could sleep and wake up and find everything in my life different," he says. "Not necessarily just the big things, like this thing with Amanda or the past with Molly. But things clearly within my power." In other words, as far as "big things" go he is helpless; even the smallest changes would require, in his mind, a fairytale awakening, some kind of miraculous intervention.

Antidotes for Hughes's powerlessness emerge variously throughout the story, the most apparent being the activity of writing. "Amanda is writing me a letter," Hughes says, seeing his lover's light on across the street, imagining her to be as distressed and sleepless as he; "somehow," he says, "it'll get into my hands later on when the real day starts." Written communication, he thinks, will provide remedy for confusion, a way of clarifying the "serious fix" he has got himself into. He imagines Amanda's husband, in fact, who has ordered his wife "out of his house," to be "awake at this moment and writing a letter to Amanda, urging reconciliation." Writing — or more precisely, the products of writing — will herald for Hughes (as does "Monday" for Leo) the "real day" that ends an interminable night of wavering resolve, of romantic ambiguity. Unfortunately, he's "never once seen a scrap of her handwriting," nor has he "written anything to her, either," and it seems unlikely that communication can or will begin now. The only "letter writer" in the story is, ironically, Molly, Hughes's ex-wife, who is mentally unstable and whose letters go completely unanswered. Hughes acknowledges writing as an antidote to disorder, sensing its prescriptive value, but he cannot or will not participate himself.

The ritual exercise of cooking, as the story's title suggests, is another remedy for emotional chaos, although it emerges in more metaphorical terms. Earlier, we learn, Hughes had broken down in a friend's kitchen, at which point his friend, Alfredo, set about to make menudo, which (as Alfredo said) would help calm him down. Hughes describes Alfredo's preparation of the dish in very precise terms:

*Tripe. He started with tripe and about a gallon of water. Then he chopped onions and added them to the water, which had started to boil. He put chorizo sausage in the pot. After that, he dropped peppercorns into the boiling water and sprinkled in some chili powder. Then came the olive oil. He opened a big can of tomato sauce and poured that in. He added cloves of garlic, some slices of white bread, salt, and lemon juice. He opened another can — it was hominy — and poured that in the pot, too. He put it all in, and then he turned the heat down and put a lid on the pot.* (348)

The hypnotic attention to detail here — the rigorous devotion to the order in which the ingredients follow each other — reminds us of Hemingway, and Nick's meal on the banks of the big two-hearted river. Like Nick en route to a "good place," Hughes benefits from the ritual of food preparation, even though he does not himself actually do any cooking. Describing the spectacle, he underlines the order intrinsic to the ceremony, suggesting that such order made his unsettled life feel a little less disordered. Even his grammar bespeaks his desire for control: all but a few of his sentences begin with the subject — Alfredo — qualified each time by what Alfredo drops into the pot, evoking not only Alfredo's mastery in cooking (in "very seriously looking after his menudo") but also the control Alfredo exerts over his world in general. "You listen to me," Alfredo tells Hughes in the kitchen, aware of his friend's present domestic distress, "I'm your family now."

But unfortunately for Hughes, Carver's restoratives are always more difficult to swallow than one might think.[13] He passes out long before the soup is ready, and, awakening the next day midafternoon and seeing that the soup is all "gone," guesses that others "have eaten it and grown calm." He assumes, significantly, that he will have to go without. Thus just as the speaker of "Boxes" is bereft of light, so is Hughes deprived of nourishment; he must forgo the pleasure of an exotic (Alfredo, not accidently, is an artist, who has "paintings of tropical birds and animals hung on every wall in his house") yet substantial means by which, symbolically speaking, to replenish himself. Albeit party to the ceremony, Hughes can't partake of the ritual substance. "I'll probably die without ever tasting menudo," he says, yet adding with that darkly distinctive late Carverian optimism, "But who knows?"[14]

In the story's last scene, still awake and more edgy than ever, Hughes applies his friend's lesson to his own life. "Alfredo, where are you?" he asks, leaving his house with a rake. "I rake our yard," he says, "every inch of it. It's important it be done right, too." The care of his lawn is clearly within his power, and the methodical activity pacifies and sustains him the way his friend's cooking earlier did. But Hughes's ritual is unfortunately as obsessive as his present state of mind. "I feel I don't have a choice in the matter any longer," he says, readying himself for his labors, and then, upon finishing his own lawn, laying into the neighbor's yard with hardly a pause. Recalling the obese man in "Fat," who, referring to his compulsive eating, admits "we have no choice," Hughes acts compulsively and furiously, externalizing his emotional autumn in a performance that lacks the serenity, and restorative potential, of ritual.[15]

Like all of Carver's outsiders, Hughes is nonetheless a survivor, and for him survival, finding his way back to the house, involves communication. Unable as he kneels in the grass to "say anything" to Mrs. Baxter (who comes out to assuage his distress), he observes Mr. Baxter, his neighbor, as he drives off to work, lifting "his hand off the steering wheel" in an ambiguous gesture as he goes by. "It could be a salute or a sign of dismissal," Hughes says. "It's a sign in any case . . . I get up and raise my hand, too — not a wave, exactly, but close to it." As tenuous as the language of the birds above in the trees ("At least I think they're calling to each other," Hughes says), this exchange nevertheless constitutes a significant transmission between a despairing Hughes and the stable, ordered world Baxter represents; Baxter is "a decent, ordinary guy — a guy you wouldn't mistake for anyone special," and yet is special in Hughes's eyes because "he has a full night's sleep behind him" and has "just embraced his wife before leaving for work." Engaging in a kind of semiotic dumb-show, Hughes makes tentative contact with the world he yearns for, a world antithetical to his own, characterized by confusion, guilt, and insomnia.

"I had an urge . . . to cross the street and rake over there," Hughes says early in the story, looking out the window at Amanda's house, "But I didn't follow through." Recharged now by his contact with Mr. Baxter, Hughes stands up and, in the story's final moments, finally follows through. "I look both ways," he says, "and then cross the street." Thanks to Carver's characteristically opaque ending, we cannot know whether Hughes means simply to rake Amanda's yard, or straighten things out between them verbally, or both, but we guess that he is moving in the right direction — toward decisive action.[16] Standing at the curb, in fact, he gets another "sign"; a motorist "gives his horn a friendly little tap" in passing. Once again, we are served affirmation and irony on the same platter, as Carver in his trademark way often dishes it up. The tap of the horn involves mistaken identity ("he must think he knows me," Hughes says), and yet while standing as one more abortive communique it also constitutes something positive as a gesture in itself. The flavor we are left with in "Menudo," then, is both sour and sweet. Sweet in that the good life shimmers as promise, sour in that the fullfulment of such promise depends on the necessarily limited choices Carver's figures possess, on the whims of a world that leaves all too little in the realm of one's power.

Like Carver's second published story, "The Father," a vignette a la Kafka dealing with loss of identity, "Blackbird Pie" is mildly expressionistic in style, a strange account of a man waking up one fine morning to find himself divorced. The story's narrator receives a written "indictment" from his wife, as he calls it, a letter mysteriously shoved under his door explaining his deficiencies as a husband. Like many of Carver's later figures, he is sensitive enough to gradually acknowledge the nature of his deficiencies, his awareness stemming, in the end, from a literal act of self-reading. Yet while he admits his own culpability in his ruined marriage, realizing at last the seriousness of past misreadings, he also admits that what he has gained in the way of illumination has come too late to be of any use.[17]

The most striking thing about this speaker is the level of his sophistication. He spends most evenings in his study devoting time to his "work," which involves, as far as we know, a great deal of reading — of history, evidently (he is a schoolteacher, it seems, maybe even a professor). His language is rhetorically far more dense, and more self-reflexive, than what we have come to expect of Carver's speakers; he exudes an intellectual precision which puts him on a more sophisticated level than the preestablished norm. But as the story demonstrates, and as this narrator finally admits, sophistication provides no guarantees of stability. In fact, as his sad course of action illustrates, sophistication can often hurt more than help. Thus much of the second half of the story takes place outside in the front yard in the fog, where he finds his wife waiting with suitcase packed, the fog enhancing both the expressionistic effect in general and the metaphorical implications of the narrator's blindness. "A fellow can't see anything in this fog," says the rancher, a man who ends up driving the wife to town and out of the narrator's life forever.

Sophisticated as he is — or because oversophistication is his tendency — the husband is a bad reader. Admitting that he didn't read his wife's letter "through in its entirety," and suspicious of the "handwriting," he says,

*What I want to say, all I want to say, is that while the sentiments expressed . . . may be my wife's, may even hold some truth — be legitimate, so to speak — the force of the accusations leveled against me is diminished, if not entirely undermined, even discredited, because she did not in fact write the letter. Or, if she did write it, then discredited by the fact that she didn't write it in her own handwriting! Such evasion is what makes men hunger for facts.* (369)

Attempting to rationalize the "indictment," the husband proves his powers of ratiocination to be as perverse as his insistence on reading the letter as a questionable document, as something to be scrutinized for authenticity rather than content. As often in the story, the narration here consists of a series of qualifications, of odd self-revisions, which interrupt the rhetorical flow of the language (not to mention the logical flow). The husband's self-indulgent method of reading is, we assume, an ongoing problem, one that ultimately paralyzes him; bad reading prevents him from acting even in ways that might illuminate, much less resurrect, the camel's back of his marriage. His overconcern for details, his "hunger for facts" (he always "scored highest on the factual tests") constitutes the greatest "evasion" in the end; remembering "names and dates" is for him, as he says, "Simple as blackbird pie," but as the reference to the nursery rhyme implies, what seems initially secure and simple on the outside, on the crust, may often contain surprises within (twenty-four dark ones, one for each year of his marriage, with wings for escape).

Good historian that he is, he returns to the letter for a second read — only to make matters worse. "Instead of beginning to read the letter through, from start to finish," he explains, "or even starting at the point where I'd stopped earlier, I took pages at random and held them under the table lamp, picking out a line here and and a line there." By reading "in snatches" he finds the "entire indictment . . . more acceptable" because it has "lost its chronology and, with it, a little of its punch." His nonchronological perusal, particularly ironic coming from a historian, provides a welter of details without a contextual sequence to give them coherence; it is no wonder that he remains, until the end, in the fog. Reducing what we imagine was originally straightforward discourse to chaos (the words and clauses he exerpts appear as "a kind of abstract," indented, in the exact middle of the narrative), the husband willfully and deliberately misreads, choosing the numbing confusion of textual inaccuracy over the painful truth of the matter. Baffled by his wife's preparations to leave, he asks her, "Can you tell me what's going on?" Knowing him only too well, the wife answers a question with a question: "You didn't read my letter, did you?" she asks. "You might have skimmed it, but you didn't read it."

Along with a manual for misreading, "Blackbird Pie" also furnishes a step-by-step guide to miscommunication — or, more accurately, non-communication. Letting "the record show," the husband describes "the evening in question": how they "ate dinner rather silently but not unpleasantly, as was [their] custom"; how he responded, or failed to respond, when his wife asked a question that was "altogether out of character for her"; how he made many mistakes. "I wonder now why on earth I didn't pursue this at the time," he muses and adds, noting the appearance of the letter under his door, "Why did I hesitate?" In one of the most painfully explanatory admissions Carver ever offers for the various defeats of his protagonists, the husband admits, "The moment was there but I hesitated. Suddenly it was too late for any decisive action. The moment had come and gone, and could not be called back." All but speechless, purely inert, he stands in the fog while his wife makes ready to leave. Recovering slightly from "a loss for words," however, he musters himself for a final confrontation:

*"The last time you wore that hat, you wore a veil with it and I held your arm. You were in mourning for your mother. And you wore a dark dress, not the dress you're wearing tonight. But those are the same high heels, I remember. Don't leave me like this . . . I don't know what I'll do."* (378)

Because "things stick" in his head, he expends his communicative energies *historicizing* his wife in terms of her clothes (which signify the death
of the marriage as far as she is concerned), rather than learning the nature of her complaints. The only thing surpassing his obsession for "facts"
is, strikingly, his self-preoccupation, "staggered" as he is by the idea that
he "*might never see her again.*" He pushes stubbornly away his muted
awareness that the marriage is dead, designating it as a history to which
he has no access.

"I'll write after I'm settled," the wife says, climbing into the pickup.
"I think I will, anyway." "Now you're talking," the deputy rejoins, adding — in the most cryptic statement of the story — "Keep all lines of
communication open." Although in his haphazard scrutiny of the letter
the husband singles out the word "*talked*" (which appears as a verb eleven
times in the first fragment of the letter), talking, like writing, is a cold
empty practice, a mere sign of proximity, not an interchange. Thus, like
the filth and debris soiling the carpet in "Collectors," and like the fallen
leaves in "Intimacy" and "Menudo," the signs of this man's decay lie at
his feet. The lawn, which has "grown shaggy, owing to a lack of interest
on [his] part," suggests that the once vital verbal link between the two,
not to mention their marriage in general, has fallen victim to neglect,
vulnerable now to strange men and horses who arrive in the night.

Alienated as Kafka's Joseph K., the husband admits that he is suddenly,
irrevocably, "outside history now." To be without a wife, he suggests, is to
be without a necessary source of self-ratification; without that influence
keeping him socially alive, he is a man with a past. Like many of Carver's
figures, people without substantial identities, he goes unnamed, a detail
not terribly noticeable in itself, until we notice that the letter begins with
"Dear" — the form of address standing by itself, no name following. The
word "Dear" operates in this story just as "Love" does in the notes Stuart
and Claire leave each other in "So Much Water So Close To Home": as
solitary signifiers such words are empty, devoid of the affection they pre-
tend to evoke, highlighting only, consciously or unconsciously, the nonexistence of the individual addressed. For another unnamed man, the unhappy son in "Boxes," the word "dear" is the key to a kind of familial
stability he cannot ever know. For the historian outside history, on the
contrary, the word is not only empty, but, given its context, semi-sarcas-

tic as well: it is both a scoff at pretended intimacy and a cipher, a symbol of his nonexistence.

In terms of self-consciousness he is not nearly as bad off as the bereft husbands of earlier volumes — as, say, Burt in "A Serious Talk," who, hoping he has "made something clear," destroys his wife's pies, cuts her phone cord and steals her ashtray, all in the interest of having "a serious talk soon." The historian-husband can at least see where he foundered, can analyze his mistakes, and learn to be a better reader by becoming more self-critical. Catching himself growing too optimistic about his wife's return, he admits, "I don't know anything about anything, and I never did." Thinking of "the consequences of the letter," attuned now to the fact of his misreading, he says, "there's far more to this than somebody's handwriting." Still "reading himself" as he narrates, he concludes, "The 'far more' has to do with subtle things" — and he goes on to puzzle out the new extrahistorical situation of his life. The "subtle things" he's beginning to grasp, now that it is sadly too late, are the simple issues of human interaction, issues whose simplicity is most apparent when we are reading and communicating well.

Unique among the last stories, "Elephant" is the closest thing to a shaggy-dog story Carver ever wrote. It is for the most part an episodic account of the verbal and written interchanges between a man and his family — a series of phone calls and letters which, as communication begins to border on exploitation, serve to alienate him from his family, who call and write only to ask him for money.[18] Living on "Easy Street," as he says, relatively successful compared to his mother, ex-wife, brother, and children, he feels obliged to his petitioners, and, inveterately a nice guy, has a hard time saying no. A victim of his own generosity and goodwill, he forgoes dentist appointments and new clothes in order to carry the "very heavy load" of his financial obligations, the demands of which increasingly dictate his life. Like "Errand," however, the story takes a turn in its final segment, throwing off the pattern of its opening pages. What begins as an inventory of demands, and a record of the narrator's reluctant compliance, ends in an awakening, and on a much more positive note than we might have expected. In other words, "Elephant" is a story that "should put paid," as Marilynne Robinson writes, "if anything ever will, to a clamor in certain quarters for a Carver story about grace and transcendence."[19]

This man's awakening is signaled by a pair of dreams, and, on the rhetorical level, by a shift in narrative sequence and tone. Describing the second of his dreams, he says, "We were on a blanket, and we were close to some water. There was a sense of satisfaction and well-being in the dream." His vision of domestic tranquility is ruptured, however, by a change of scenery — a flashback of his drinking days and of a violent encounter he had with his son. "I was kicking out the window of my son's car," he says, describing the dream, "and threatening his life, as I did once, a long time ago." An uncontrollable subconscious phenomenon, a nightmare, reminds him of a particularly out-of-control time in his past, a part of himself he now holds in check, carefully under control. The dream also emphasizes the tensions he presently experiences with the men in his life, with the man his daughter is living with (whom he also "threatened to kill") and with his brother, in a sense the occasion for the story ("I knew it was a mistake to let my brother have the money," the story's opening sentence reads), the only one of his supportees he isn't in any sense obliged to satisfy. But the speaker's fears are mollified even as they are recalled, both by the remaining content of his dreams and, slightly later, by his connection with George — by the union we see in the final moments of the story.

"In the first dream," the narrator explains, "my dad was alive once more, and he was giving me a ride on his shoulders." The dreamer here aligns himself with his father in an odd way, and his own present circumstances with those of his father's past:

I was this little kid, maybe five or six years old. Get up here, he said, and he took me by the hands and swung me onto his shoulders. I was high off the ground, but I wasn't afraid. He was holding on to me. We were holding on to each other. Then he began to move down the sidewalk . . . You can let go, he said, I've got you. You won't fall. When he said that, I became aware of the strong grip of his hands around my ankles. Then I did let go. I turned loose and held my arms out on either side of me. I kept them out there like that for balance. My dad went on walking while I rode on his shoulders. I pretended he was an elephant. I don't know where we were going. Maybe we were going to the store, or else to the park so he could push me in the swing. (361)

Consciously or otherwise, he draws out the likeness between his father and himself, likening the way his father once supported him (on "his shoulders") to the way he is himself financially supporting his own as well as his father's family now. Like the "elephant" he imagines his father to be, extra strong, extra benevolent, he plods along now bearing his family, and with elephantine patience has not let them fall. "I put more checks in the mail," he says, concluding his first tally of obligations. "Then I held my breath and waited." His mention of "the swing" in his dream further echoes his daughter's comments about his grandchildren, who had drawn "pictures of the swing sets" at the motel he'd stayed in when he visited, and reinforces his sense of obligation; though they ask nothing of him, his grandchildren depend on him, too.

Standing beside the highway on his way to work, he enacts a gesture he remembers from the dream, raising his arms and holding them out "for balance" as he had on his father's shoulders. Unlike the embraces in "Boxes," or the sign language in "Menudo," this gesture is uniquely personal, a gesture aimed at equanimity, at psychic equilibrium on the part of the dreamer. "[S]tanding there like that, like a goof" on the roadside, he hopes to "balance" the past with the present; to offset old memories of drunkenness with his more recent sobriety, to mitigate residual guilt by weighing it against those compensatory tokens of restoration he has lately, ungrudgingly, bestowed. In another sense, he seeks to balance his meager successes with the individual failures of his kin, and balance his resistance to circumstances in general with, as the story's ending suggests, unconditional acceptance.

Like the historian in "Blackbird Pie," this man reassesses his predicament, examining his motives in a kind of "self-reading" now familiar to us, knowing as we do the figures and situations of the last stories. "[A]ll of a sudden," he says, "I could imagine how it must have sounded to my family when I'd threatened them with a move to Australia . . . Now, thinking about their laughter, I had to laugh, too. Ha, ha, ha. That was exactly the sound I made there at the table— ha, ha, ha — as if I'd read somewhere how to laugh." In a curious way an audience unto himself, auditing not only his personal motivations but the very sound of his voice, he begins to see his world — not unlike the man in "Cathedral" — from a different perspective. Engaging in reflective self-dissociation, he realizes that unlike birds who move "from one part of the valley to another," he can't (or doesn't actually want to) fly off to escape the crush of obligation. He understands, finally, that "Australia" is an empty threat, pure self-deception, understanding in a way that Donna in "Vitamins" cannot, her heart desperately set on the illusory glimmer of "Portland," and as Leo in "What Is It?" cannot, banking his few remaining hopes on an equally illusory day of the week. "[O]nce I understood this," the man in "Elephant" says, sitting in his kitchen over morning coffee, "once I understood I wouldn't be going there — or anywhere else, for that matter — I began to feel better." As George notes slightly later, his friend is indeed "in training"; he is a blue-collar existential athlete of sorts, a late twentieth century Sisyphus learning the hard way that toil and daily obligation is only as bad as you make it, contingent on perspective and the set of one's mind. Wishing the best for each member of his family — taking a final inventory as he walks — he says he feels he has "the right to whistle if [he] wanted to," implying that there are always degrees of freedom within constraint, and that there is usually "lots to hope for."

"'Hey, get in, buddy,'" George says, pulling up in his car — cutting short, one tends to think, the narrator's newfound freedom, the release accompanying that sudden, wholesale acceptance of his "load." George's intrusion seems to disrupt the serenity of the narrator's mood, and his address smacks of abduction, but his presence allows for yet another release in the form of the car — an extension, in fact, of the narrator's newfound freedom.[20] "I borrowed some money and had this baby overhauled," George explains while accelerating (toying with his unlit cigar, he is the proud father of a "baby" that costs him dearly — he's had to borrow to support it). George has discovered, as his coworker has, that not only do responsibilities and obligations sometimes fail to drag one down, they even afford uncanny liberty. Identifying closely with George — they share an identical laugh ("ha, ha, ha") — the narrator directs his final question as much to himself as to his friend: "What are you waiting for, George?" he asks, encouraging George to step on the gas. He has begun to learn at last just how futile "waiting" and holding one's breath can be, and how unnecessary. Although they face the company time clock soon, he and George streak "down that road in [George's] big unpaid-for car," proving that even the smallest freedoms can be exhilarating, and that borrowed freedom is freedom nevertheless — is for some of us, for all of Carver's characters, the only real freedom we know.

In "Whoever Was Using This Bed" Carver falls back on a few familiar devices — the wrong number caller, insomnia — and in the process reinvigorates them, perhaps because the "obsession" to which he links them is new: the subject of human mortality. Death has been present in Carver's work from the beginning, of course, but only obliquely — only, as Tobias Wolff observes, as "an atmosphere of malign possibility." But in "his last stories and poems," Wolff writes, Carver "dragged the beast out of the corner and stared it in the face."[21] While the poems deal much more specifically, and autobiographically, with the "beast" ("What the Doctor Said" comes to mind, the title saying it all), "Whoever" provides a humorous, comprehensive look at human powerlessness in the face of oblivion, as well as at our strategies for compensating for such debility.[22]

"The call comes in the middle of the night," says Jack, the story's narrator, "and it nearly scares us to death." Jack and his wife Iris are flung into wakefulness by a wrong number caller, and, momentarily terrified, are prompted to conversation. Too jumpy to go back to sleep, they talk away the rest of the night, their conversation occupying most of the story. Focusing at first on the subject of sickness, their conversation moves eventually to terminal illness and dying, yet their dialogue is so unfocused that a good amount of talking goes on while not a whole lot gets said. At one point, when Iris grows fearful at the idea of living like a "vegetable," Jack tries to comfort her, saying,

"It won't happen to us. It won't," I say. "Don't worry about any of it, okay? We're fine, Iris, and we're going to stay fine. In any case, that time's a long time off. Hey, I love you. We love each other, don't we? That's the important thing. That's what counts. Don't worry, honey." (327)

Endeavoring to calm his wife, Jack's deeper concerns — concerns as grave as Iris's — are given away by his language. The repetition of words ("won't," "worry," "fine," "love"), not to mention the urgency of his tone, betray that he is trying to convince himself as much as her of their safety. Considering the rhetorical economy of the story — one of Carver's fullest, for sure, and the most dialogue-packed — it is hard not to see talking itself as a reaction to menace, to the threat of personal suffering and death. In a similar sense, "What We Talk About When We Talk About Love" presents a symposium on a subject so elusive and powerful that its discoursers can only talk around it, and are left literally in the dark in the end. Jack and Iris, however, deal with a much darker subject, a subject even more awesome and slippery, talking and talking in an attempt as much to ward it off as to understand it fully.

Exhausted and edgy the following day, Jack says, "I feel as if I've come to a place I never thought I'd have come to . . . It's a strange place. It's a place where a little harmless dreaming and then some sleepy, early-morning talk has led me into considerations of death and annihilation." The "place" Jack speaks of, that vertiginous realm of existential reflection, is one he both enters with words and, with varying degrees of anxiety, covers over with words, trying to bury it again as best he can. It is a place both familiar and starkly alien, a place he finds himself in suddenly, signaled by a phone call, itself a form of verbal transmission. The caller's desperation, infecting Jack and Iris in turn, is grounded in a desire identical to theirs: the desire to be saturated with language. "Bud," she pleads, unable to believe that Jack is Jack and not Bud, "talk to me, please."

"She's more on my side than her own side," Jack says of his wife, surveying the bed as he returns from the phone — a statement echoing in the halls of Carver's canon, from Nan's despairing glimpse of her husband's "arm flung out across her side of the bed" in "The Student's Wife," to the transplanted bedroom set in "Why Don't You Dance?," featuring "his side" and "her side," to Hughes's unhappy observation of his wife "scrunched on to about ten inches of mattress," sleeping "on her side of the bed."[23] Such echoes reemphasize the power politics of the bedroom, the division drawn out in lines of romantic scrimmage. Like Nan, Jack is not so much troubled by distance and separation as he is by proximity. The sheer physicality of his wife's presence on his side of the bed is symptomatic of larger problems involving psychic space, problems having to do with what is ultimately the greatest freedom one can imagine: freedom of choosing life over death. The question of whether to give one's spouse authority to "pull the plug" evokes, as one reviewer says of Jack and Iris, "the extreme of intimacy their marriage implies."[24] Similarly in "Proposal," a late poem about Ray and Tess's marriage (which took place just months before Carver's death), the speaker exclaims, "Oh lovely, oh lethal entanglements," musing on a film romance in which Betty Davis kills her ex-lover. In another poem, "Wake Up" (also from *Waterfall*), a couple plays morbid games in the dungeon of Zurich's Kyborg Castle, the speaker placing his "head on the block" while his mate simulates the blow of decapitation with her hand.[25]

This is this kind of authority that Jack, who speaks earlier of a time he and his wife were "fistfighting" in their sleep, resists. "Don't unplug me," he says, having mulled too long over the question of the life-support machines. "Leave me hooked up just as long as possible," he insists. "Right to the bitter end."[26] Not unlike others in Carver country, Jack clings to what little control he has in death's kingdom, the realm of the uncontrollable. Like Hughes, rake in hand, facing the "big things" in his life by focusing on small things first, Jack needs the order of a well-made bed to offset the vast disorder of sleep's second self, a thing terrifyingly beyond the scope of personal jurisdiction. For him, the "strange place" they arrive at in their conversation precludes a return to preexistentialist innocence — it is like reading Sartre and then trying to forget about him. "I know I won't ever look at this bed again," Jack says, noticing the disarray of sheets and blankets around him, "without remembering it like this."

Try as he might, then, Jack is not the master of his world he would like to think he is. The story closes with one last phone call, and with Jack reproaching the caller for rudeness; but as he scolds he finds the words suddenly taken out of his mouth: his wife unplugs the phone. "[W]hile I'm trying to tell all this to the woman," he says, "while I'm trying to make myself understood, my wife moves quickly and bends over, and that's it. The line goes dead, and I can't hear anything." Once again, Jack tries to "tell all" in an effort to fill up the unknown, trying to cover over oblivion with words, and now, emblematically speaking, his worst fears suddenly come true. With the rhetorical finality of "that's it," accompanied by the adroitly placed cliche "dead" and the reverberating silence evoked by the final clause, Jack's powerlessness could not be more gravely emphasized. With no choice left in the matter, Jack's "extreme of intimacy" is embodied by his noticeable lack of autonomy. In "Blackbird Pie" being single spells out a frightening loss of identity, but in this story things are just the opposite — overintimacy in marriage makes for the dissolution of personal integrity, and a tendency toward lapsing into nonidentity.

"It looks like whoever was using this bed left in a hurry," Jack observes, underlining not only his obsessiveness about a tidy bed but also, evoked by the indefiniteness of the word "whoever," the kind of anonymity he senses arising of confrontations with the incomprehensible, with forces larger and more powerful than he can begin to imagine. "We could have been anybody," Hughes says on a similar note, describing his meeting with Amanda in the coffee shop, caught up in the pervasiveness and randomness of love's victimizations. Reducing himself and his wife alike to the indefinite "whoever," Jack suggests how little control we all have in everything, and how, talk as much as we like, we come and go in a hurry.

Carver's last story, "Errand," treats the subject of mortality much more directly, dealing with it in terms of his own life and its connection to art. In this story Carver aligns himself, and his image of himself as an artist, with Chekov, who died similarly of a lung condition. (Although Carver wrote the story, as he intimates at one point, months before he knew the severity of his illness, it nevertheless stands — unconscious or not — as an exploration of, if not a preparation for, his own premature death.)[27] To longtime devotees of Carver it is hardly a surprise to find Chekov serving as guide. Chekov was a primary mentor for Carver, a figure who had from the very beginning led Carver through ordeals and crises — emotional as well as artistic. More than twenty years before, Carver had published "Winter Insomnia," a poem in which he writes, "The mind is sick tonight/ It wishes Chekov were here to minister/ Something — three drops of valerian, a glass/ Of rose water/ anything, it wouldn't matter."[28] Chekov was as much a spiritual doctor for Carver as a literary model, a wellspring of insights intrinsic to his own life and work. ("And then suddenly," reads the Chekov exerpt Carver kept pinned above his desk, "everything became clear to him.")[29] Introducing A New Path To The Waterfall, Tess Gallagher describes Chekov's stories — and their partial incorporation into the volume — as "integral to [her and Ray's] spiritual survival," observing how the stories helped in completing not only a book but a life.[30]

"Errand," then, is not so much a departure from as the continuation of a trend. However, the style of the story constitutes a monumental departure from the norm, categorizable more along the lines of Dostoevsky (a screenplay, a bittersweet tribute to the master, cowritten by Gallagher and Carver) than within the normal context of his canon. "Errand" is in part a semi-historical documentary of Chekov's last years. It records the progression of his illness, along with a meticulous account of the hours preceding and succeeding the moment of his death.[31] Most striking, perhaps, is the conspicuous transformation of documentary into fiction in the story's final pages: what begins as a baldly historical account of incidents and dates culminates in a dreamy, hyper-detailed description of a fictional exchange between Chekov's widow and a bellhop.

Just as Chekov, as Carver writes in the story, "continually tried to minimalize the seriousness of his condition," behaving as though he might "throw off the disease"; and just as, despite the worsening of his symptoms, he "didn't stop" writing, so Carver kept the development of his illness a secret and, as Gallagher writes, "kept working, planning, believing in the importance of the time he had left . . . believing that he might, through some loop in fate, even get out." In this sense "Errand" is Carver's way of "practicing" for death (as Gallagher describes the decapitation games in "Wake Up"), of going through the motions, of letting imagination precede physical reality, so that his last hours in the world might come to seem as full of grace and control he envisioned those of his mentor to be.[32] Most importantly, by aligning himself with the Russian writer, Carver displaces his own impending death, exploring its implications in a way that, recalling Jack and Iris's interminable chitchat, confronts reality in the act of displacing it — and then takes displacement one step further by focusing on characters peripheral to the story's subject. If at first glance "Errand" seems as dissimilar to earlier stories in subject as in style, a close look reveals that Carver is still operating as he always has. Reflecting here more than ever the concerns of their creator, characters struggle for control in circumstances where individual control has been shaken, particularly toward the end of the story. With death now an adversary, these figures struggle harder than ever, their compensatory strategies, their footholds against the unknown, as distinctive as they are familiar to readers of Carver.

Ceremony is the main foothold, evidenced in the drinking of champagne, in Olga's vigil, and in her rigorous instructions to the bellhop regarding a mortician. Ceremony lends structure to the unstructurable, to chaos arriving in the unseeable guise of death. It allows Olga, reflecting later upon her hours at the dead man's bedside, to write, "There was only beauty, peace, and the grandeur of death."[33] Hoping to avoid raising a "commotion" among the townspeople, she bids the boy to hold his tongue, asking him to seek out a mortician who, like the "great artist" he is about to bury, takes "great pains in his work" — someone who is, generally speaking, "a man of restraint and bearing." Obsessed with the orderliness of the procedure, she instructs him to move "without any unbecoming haste" and comport "himself at all times in as dignified a manner as possible." For Olga, ceremony stabilizes a world fallen into disarray. Poised at the intersection of life and chaos, ritual activity is her guiding impulse, a series of signposts pointing the way back to life. "The worst is over," she tells the boy, and then delineates for him, in amazingly precise terms, the nature of his errand.

Because Carver's world is as complex as it is, the intrusion of the bellhop into the somber setting of the deathbed represents both an enhancement of and a fly in the ointment in the orderly tableau we find on the surface. With his "wrinkled" clothes and hair "standing up," the boy's presence evokes vibrant youthfulness and naive vitality, associated as he is with the cork whose "festive pop" the doctor tries to suppress while opening the champagne (it is later ejected haphazardly into the room). "[T]hinking of the cork," the boy finds it difficult to concentrate on Olga's directions, simultaneously caught up — as Carver himself seems to be — in the horror and the fascinating peculiarity of his circumstances. (He was earlier awakened, we recall, as were Iris and Jack, when "the phone . . . clamored," responding to the ring of death in the night.) He chooses "not to look again in the direction of the other room," where death's visage lies, and, perhaps overcompensating for his fear, lets himself fall silently into the stream of Olga's imagination, into her verbal performance, which is both firmly solidified by the nature of its content (ritual) and hypnotically vibrant with detail. Inert as he might seem, however, the boy is not paralyzed. In the otherwise "tidy" and "undisturbed" room, the cork is the sole object out of place, so, like Hughes on the verge of crossing the street, he reaches out, balancing precariously — he's still holding the vase — and closes it in his hand. The small things around him are indeed still within his power, if for no other reason than their being part of his duty, his charge.

In this tale-as-final-testament, Carver performs a similar balancing act. Like the young bellhop, nervous, observant, trembling with wonder, he confronts death by glancing quickly and then turning away. Through our imaginations, he suggests — and through our ceremonies, the products of our imaginations — we transcend oblivion: we daydream, we tidy the room. As Tess Gallagher notes, comparing "Errand" to one of Carver's recent biographical pieces, "it is the ordinary moment which illuminates the most extraordinary things."[34] The moment the boy reaches for the cork, ordinary as it might seem, is a moment epitomizing in one tiny gesture our capacities for preserving dignity and "bearing" in the face of overwhelming calamity. Casting the net of self over history, making it his own, Carver creates a vision that is as much about life as about the death he intends to represent.

"I needed to figure out how to breathe life into actions that were merely suggested or not given moment in the biographical telling," Carver says, explaining how the story came together. "I saw that I needed to set my imagination free and simply invent within the confines of the story."[35] The creative imagination, in this sense, allows him to "breath life" into something initially fixed, set in the textual concrete of history, albeit capable of expansion, as in "The Bath." "[A]ll stories," Carver says in a poem (citing Hemingway), "if continued far enough/end in death. Truly."[36] But even as this grim motto is asserted in "Errand," it is not grimness that we come away with but triumph, a sense of the triumphs of imagination, the limited yet inspirational victories of the human mind over cessation. Just as the boy "Without looking down" reaches for the cork, Carver the writer, poised at the edge of the void but gazing back at humanity, reaches for the odd detail, illustrating how eternity can reside in an extraordinarily ordinary moment. Through our stories and our storytelling, he suggests, we find in even the most dire times freedom in "confines," in preconceived structures and circumstance. It is the writer's task, he also suggests, to convey this truth both in living and in dying, both in and beyond art.

If "Errand" is Carver's personalized statement on a writer's working relationship with death, then "Intimacy" is his statement on the subject of his aesthetic. If "Errand," that is, explores the ways in which an artist copes with mortality, then "Intimacy" explores the more technical aspects of coping: it suggests how Carver erected his own peculiar system of order amidst the disorder he experienced, as both an artist and a man. Pushing beyond the frame-tale obliqueness of "Put Yourself in My Shoes," his only other story concerned specifically with writing, and beyond the fairly generic distinctions he makes in "On Writing" and in autobiographical issues of "Fires," the intimations of "Intimacy" (along with a number of prose poems in *A New Path to the Waterfall*, which illuminate certain issues pertaining to his poetry) provide an insider's take on Carver's writerly world, refracted though they are in that always tenuous, semi-unreliable medium of prose fiction.[37] Emphasizing again the "opening up" in the work, illuminating yet another dimension of Carver's multi-textured, multi-sided expansion, the story sheds new light on the darkness of Carver's obsessions, and on the deeper implications of style.

"Intimacy" presents the brief meeting of a successful fiction writer with his ex-wife, a woman with whom, to say the least, he is on unsteady terms. The husband revisits a landscape — the house they once shared, it would seem — that is as psychological as it is physical: "Make no mistake," he tells us, "I feel I'm home." The story consists of a mainly one-sided dialogue in which ex-wife berates husband, who responds only intermittently. After upbraiding him for his "betrayal," for throwing her away, she launches into his writing, complaining that he misrepresents the circumstances of a past to which she is specifically party. He is forever "dredging up that old business," she insists; he exploits the "hard times" and "the bad times," which, as far as she is concerned, are "low, shameful things," overlooking the positive side of the past. In one of his rare revelatory remarks, the writer-husband responds: "I admit I hold to the dark view of things," he tells her. In one of the more dramatic moments of the story, affected by his ex-wife's condemnations, he kneels on the floor and, in an odd, inarticulate gesture of placation, takes "the hem of her dress," remaining there "stuck to the floor" until she in a sense exonerates him for past actions ("She says, I forgive you") and insists he get up and leave.

Willing to do "Anything to avoid a fuss," as his ex-wife observes, lashed soundly by her tongue, he takes a good deal of abuse — abuse that, given the story's general premise, seems oddly necessary to him. The hard times and bad times of his fiction, we learn, are intrinsic to memories of his old life (and, to an extent, to this woman he married, a human storehouse of details concerning those earlier days). Kneeling submissively before her, curiously passive, he is dominated by his "material," a domination mirrored even on the level of story's rhetoric: two-thirds of the paragraphs begin with "She says." He returns as much to settle unfinished emotional business as to delve into his past, and to be bowed again by that past. Successful now in his own right, more comfortable and secure than before, he seeks the "old hurts," as his ex-wife calls them; riding his own "private hobby horse," he exploits the oppressiveness he knows from earlier days, the darkness of that previous life. Repeated exposure (to the past and to the past's dictating forces) sustains him, the story suggests, makes his art possible, allowing him access to the constraints of the world he creates and the constraints which have, in a very real sense, created him. "Maybe you'll be back sometime," his ex-wife says as he goes out the door, "and maybe you won't. This'll wear off, you know. Pretty soon you'll start feeling bad again. Maybe it'll make a good story." A "good story," in this writer's terms, is in some way contingent, we suppose — even if we distrust the wife — on "feeling bad." His heart, the wellspring of his work, is, as the ex-wife puts it, a "dark forest," or, in less lenient terms, "a garbage pail." Those necessary rediscoveries of heart — periodic returns to the center of immense darkness, to the bottom of the bucket — depend to some degree on enforced captivity, on submission, and — always important in Carver's book — on humility.

In perhaps the only truly "intimate" moment of the tale, the ex-wife, drawing extremely close to his face, says, "You just tell it like you have to, and forget the rest. Like always." Continuing, she says, "There, I've done it. You're free, aren't you? At least you think you are anyway. Free at last." Her half-hearted blessing evokes an odd double message: she tells her ex-husband he is "free" to do as he likes, to write what he wants, but implies that freedom, at least as far as they are concerned, is merely a construction of the mind. Leaving, he goes down the sidewalk and notices "Some kids," observing that "they aren't [his] kids, and they aren't her kids either," suggesting that the past (flesh and blood, presumably, in this case) will bind them forever. Intimacy, the story suggests — even intimacy gone sour, thanks to prolonged human contact — is always painfully complex, even in moribund form. Freedom, in terms of emotional ties and life after marriage, does not in this sense truly exist. Again, natural decay creeps into the picture, this time in the story's last sentences:

*There are these leaves everywhere, even in the gutters. Piles of leaves wherever I look. They're falling off the limbs as I walk. I can't take a step without putting my shoe into leaves. Somebody ought to make an effort here. Somebody ought to get a rake and take care of this.* (337)

The disorderliness of the natural world — as it does elsewhere in Carver, for all its transfiguration and decay — functions as a trope for the psychic state of the speaker. Estranged now from his wife and perhaps from his children, the accumulated debris at his feet represents both the tangible nature of familial ruin, of "tragedy," as she calls it, and the terribly natural degree of its inevitability. He wades, metaphorically, through the turmoil of his past — not unlike a man in a poem appearing two years earlier in *Ultramarine:* "Everywhere he went that day," we hear, "he walked/in his own past. Kicked through piles/of memories."[38] Articulating the husband-writer's desire for renewal involves, aptly enough, indefinite language, the "Somebody" who ought to come with a rake. Echoing an earlier statement he made, the auxiliary verb "ought" underlines the obligation he feels — and then displaces, hoping to see things in his life turn eventually more tidy. But because he implicates himself in his own indefiniteness, "Somebody" seems at best a small hedge against chaos, one serving only, we guess, to compound his hopelessness.

Still, he will presumably "take care of this" as he always does — as Carver has already, in fact — by writing the story. The pen is indeed mightier than the rake, and the husband-writer's conscience may be lightened by more than his ex-wife's partial forgiveness and mixed blessing, since chances are he will be redeemed to some extent by a "good story," one drawing him into better terms with the past, if not with himself. (That we are actually reading this story, a story about redemption and writing, indirectly implies this redemption.) As in the lighter tales of *Cathedral* — "Where I'm Calling From," especially, and "A Small, Good

Thing" and "Fever" — suggest, telling serves, if only in the form of glow-ing potential, as release from captivity, release which comes of exploring one's past through acts of refinement, through the modifying, control-ling, and sharpening (and darkening, if need be) of artistic vision. We write to understand, Carver implies, and through understanding we find new kinds of freedom, loosening the grip of the past even as we replay and absorb it (but never escape; "Why don't you wipe the blackboard clean and see what you have left after that?" the ex-wife asks. "Why don't you start with a clean slate? See how far that gets you"). Winking at us at times in the story, at play in the fields of the metafictional, Carver sheds new light on the dark inner realm of his craft, spelling out the relation of one writer to the bulk of his past. "Just let them come around here," the ex-wife exclaims, referring to her husband's critics and admirers, "and I'll give them an earful." As critics and admirers of Carver, as partakers of a new kind of intimacy, we are all ears.

"He never left those memories of the bad times, family breakup, alco-hol, hardscrabble jobs," William Stafford writes, not long after Carver died in Port Angeles.[39] Indeed, as an artist Carver was nourished by such memories, as "Intimacy" suggests, and the last stories, with their new and old obsessions alike, bring on the immediacy and vitality of those memories, be they imagined or real, with renewed intensity and fresh-ness. While a few may argue, as does a reviewer of A New Path to the Wa-terfall, that "Carver takes his reader on a final journey that leads in one direction, downward into darkness," most will agree that the forest we enter in his final work, black as it seems at times, is not without paths leading out, paths pointing toward light, if not toward affirmation then at least toward a crossroads, a place portending better times, the better life.[40] In what often seems an oppressive, hostile, overdetermined world, Carver's figures persist, struggling to stay alive in every sense of the phrase. "At the heart of their emptiness," Pierre Lepape notes of Carver's last characters, "at the very source of their weakness, a small fragment of hope arises that allows the characters to continue living and to nudge themselves further along the dead-end roads of their lives."[41] Survival is necessarily as much the key in the end as it was in the beginning. Or, as Carver himself says of his later work:

*The vision now, today, is, I suppose, more hopeful than it was. But for the most part, things don't work out for the characters in the stories. Things perish. Ideas and ideals and people's goals and visions — they perish. But sometimes, oftentimes, the people themselves don't perish. They have to pull up their socks and go on.*[42]

Many critics, European ones in particular, choose to see Carver's universe, his cast of imperishable blue-collar survivors, as symptomatic of a national problem, a malaise cropping up in late twentieth century American literature, especially in the short story. John Clute, among others, sees the work of American "minimalist" writers — Carver, Ford and Wolff, specifically — as bearing "witness to an entire continent in distress."[43] Carver himself conceded the point, however grudgingly: "I write oftentimes about working-class people," he says, "and the dark side of Reagan's America. So in that regard I suppose the stories can be read as a criticism, an indictment. But that has to come from the outside."[44] The "dark side," it would seem — approaching as we do, with respectful distance, from the outside — is for Carver at once a sociological phenomenon involving the disinheritance of a whole class of people, and, as "Intimacy" suggests, an artistic vision for representing such disheritance. His literary and spiritual alignment with Chekov, whose stories tend to deal with "submerged populations," as Carver describes them, takes on noticeable social dimensions in this light, dimensions illuminated even more fully by Carver's inclusion of several (formerly) East Block poets (Seifert, Transtromer, Milosz) in his last book of poems.[45] Carver's interest in artists oppressed in overt ways — in the controlling strictures of dictatorial governments, say — enhanced and extended his understanding of people in "free" societies, people whose lives are similarly oppressed, however covertly.

If America is a country where, as John Cheever writes, "we are haunted by a dream of excellence" — where even modestly successful suburbanites, as Cheever paints them, are bewildered by impulses they cannot embody and baffled by residual, inscrutable longings — then Carver's America, held up against Cheever's, greatly magnifies the symptoms of our haunted condition. Carver's figures are haunted by the dream of a dream, or by something even more tenuous than that. They are be-

wildered not so much by vague longings and failed dreams as by the utter *absence* of a dream, by the black hole resulting from the dream's disap-
pearance. Carver's characters find themselves consistently locked out and
in the dark, without history, existing always in that "strange place" where
fear and confusion abounds and alienation is a fact of existence. Carver's
social awareness picks up where Chekov and Cheever left off, emphasizing above all else how much harder it is getting for some of us to pull up
our socks and go on. It is no wonder that the British, who often seem
more aware of our submerged populations than we are, link Carver so
firmly with his mentor, that they dubbed him "the American Chekov" —
the epithet appeared in the *London Times* the day after he died.[46]

Though never themselves inclined toward the political, the stories explore in their subtle and various ways that "dark side" of American affluence, and do so with uncanny power, presenting *en sum*, in the words of
one critic, an "aesthetic of failure."[47] The last stories, redolent with characters of unprecedented awareness, serve to heighten this sense of collective and ongoing dispossession; the fact that characters are now more articulate than before, that they now sense, if dimly, the contours of their
"deprivation" (to use Irving Howe's word), only makes their losses that
much more penetrating. Thanks to their persistence, to discoveries they
make about themselves and about others, to the integrity they maintain as
their worlds collapse, Carver's characters are never merely symptomatic,
never simply pathetic, but are heroically and tragically so.

Wary of the idea of artists acting as mouthpieces or spokespeople for
nations and societies, Carver is nonetheless quick to assert the need for
communication in artistic enterprises. "[A]rt is a linking between
people," Carver says in an interview, "the creator and the consumer. Art
is not self-expression, it is communication, and I am interested in communication."[48] While expressing doubts about the capacities of fiction for
instilling moral change in the populace, he nevertheless concedes its potential for imparting insight. "Maybe writing fiction about particular
kinds of people living particular kinds of lives," he says, "will allow certain areas of life to be understood a little better than they were understood before."[49]

"Good fiction," as he puts it even more vividly, "is partly a bringing
of the news from one world to another."[50] A crucial function of Carver's

storytelling is bringing the news of an especially formidable darkness into the light, begging if not for antidotes then at least for our recognition of that darker world's existence. Carver's ladder starts, as did Yeats's, in the "rag and bone shop of the heart," that garbage pail of human experience. Reaching deep, he draws out in painstaking detail the implications of a painful, collective captivity, and if he fails to move us to action he certainly moves us, as he has moved the characters of these stories, to reflection, to inventory, and, if we are careful and lucky, to understanding. It is as much, he seems to suggest, as we can expect of art, and of the short story. The best stories of our time, Carver writes as an editor, "throw some light on what it is that makes us and keeps us, often against great odds, recognizably human."[51]

# Notes

## INTRODUCTION

1  Skenazy, "Life in Limbo," 79.

2  Fisketjon, "Normal Nightmares," 132.

3  McInerney, "A Still, Small Voice," 25.

4  Cheever, "The Death of Justina," in *The Stories of John Cheever*, 432.

5  Skenazy, "Life in Limbo," 80.

6  Howe, "Stories," 43.

7  Carver, Interview with Kasia Boddy, 16. For a taste of the worst conservative critics, see Eichman, "Please Be Quiet," 86–89.

8  Herzinger, "Introduction," 7, 14, 19. I am particularly indebted to Herzinger and his ground-breaking essay in my reflections here, as well as in other sections of this study.

9  Skenazy, "Life in Limbo," 81.

10 Barth, "A Few Words," 14. As one might expect, another "correction" in the cycle has already begun; in the short stories of Lee K. Abbott and Ethan Canin, for instance, a counterreaction is being embodied in a brand of postminimalist fullness, both in the swelling rhetoric of the prose (Abbott) and in a return to highly developed metaphor (Canin). See Pope, "The Post-Minimalist American Short Story," 331–42.

11 In a substantial way, of course, realism has been with us all along — in the thought-swollen reveries of Saul Bellow and in John Updike's shimmering surfaces, as well as in the oddly classical realism of John Gardner, Carver's teacher; hence the advent of "minimalism" can be classified as the continuation and distillation of one trend almost as easily as it can be termed a reaction to another.

12 Barth enumerates a number of additional "conditions" to which he supposes the advent of literary "minimalism" can be attributed, which include the Vietnam War, the energy crisis of 1973–76, a decline in literacy, a dwindling "readerly attention span," and the "all but inescapable hyperbole of American advertising." Some of the suppositions here, it seems to me, are less plausible than others. See Barth, "A Few Words."

13 Carver's adherence to modernist principles is strikingly epitomized by Pound's credo, "Fundamental accuracy of statement is the ONE sole morality of writing," which Carver transcibed onto a three-by-five card and kept taped to the wall beside his desk; his reverence for Chekov — the man who (along with Joyce and others) first overhauled the short story — is yet another expression of Carver's modernist insistence on "making it new." See Carver, "On Writing," in Fires, 13–18.

14 See especially McInerney, "A Still, Small Voice."

15 Carver, contribution to "A Symposium of Contemporary American Fiction," 711.

16 For the best essays to date on Carver's poetry, see Gallagher, Introduction to A New Path to the Waterfall, and Kuzma, "Ultramarine."

17 Carver, Interview with Michael Schumacher, 18.

18 Gardner, On Moral Fiction, 6.

19 Carver, ed., Introduction to Best American Short Stories 1986, xiv.

CHAPTER ONE

1 Wood, "Stories," 34; Stull, "Beyond Hopelessville," 2.

2 Stull, DLB Yearbook 1988, 206. Citing Camus, Carver refers here to the stories of William Kittredge, his statement appearing in an introduction to Kittredge's We Are Not In This Together, ix.

3 Wood, "Stories," 34.

4 At Night the Salmon Move, 44.

5 Stull, "Beyond Hopelessville," 1.

6 Wood, "Stories," 1.

7 Interview with Mona Simpson, 207.

8 Saltzman, Understanding Raymond Carver, 22.

9 Will You Please Be Quiet, Please?, 7.

10  Stull, DLB Yearbook 1988, 207.

11  Beattie, Ann, "Carver's Furious Seasons," 178.

12  Boxer, "Art of Raymond Carver," 76.

13  Flower, "Fiction Chronicle," 281.

14  Boxer, "Art of Raymond Carver," 77.

15  Boxer, "Art of Raymond Carver," 77.

16  For alternative and equally fascinating possibilities in fictive obesity, see Miller, "Poets of Reality," 187–89; see also DeMarinis, "Life Between Meals," in Under the Wheat, 81–101.

17  At Night the Salmon Move, 11.

18  Saltzman, Understanding Raymond Carver, 24.

19  Wood, "Stories," 1, 34.

20  Stull, DLB Yearbook 1988, 207.

21  Boxer, "Art of Raymond Carver," 75.

22  Fisketjon, "Normal Nightmares," 132.

23  "Limits," Ultramarine, 37.

24  Boxer, "Art of Raymond Carver," 85.

25  Mars-Jones, "Words," 76.

26  Beattie, "Carver's Furious Seasons," 181.

27  Boxer, "Art of Raymond Carver," 88–89.

28  "[A]ctually," Tess Gallagher informs me, by way of qualification, "it began in What We Talk About, but because of severe editing by Gordon Lish, it did not become visible until Cathedral."

29  A New Path to the Waterfall, 14.

30  Stephen Spender, epigraph to "The Author of her Misfortune," in Carver, Ultramarine, 51.

31  Carver, Interview with Mona Simpson, 207.

32  Carver, Interview with William Stull, 153.

33  Carver, Interview with Kasia Boddy, 16.

34  Stull, DLB Yearbook 1984, 241.

35  "The Sensitive Girl," Ultramarine, 38–39.

CHAPTER TWO

1   Stone, 58; Coover, "Fiction and America," 7; Bell, "Less is Less," 67; Atlas,
    "Less is Less," 96, 98.

2   Eichman, Erich, "Please Be Quiet," 86; Bell, "Less is Less," 67; Gorra,
    "Laughter and Bloodshed," 155; Houston, "A Stunning Inarticulateness," 23;
    Clute, "Word-Danger," 572; Stull, DLB Yearbook 1984, 240; Mars-Jones,
    "Words," 76; Phillips, "Secret Places," 77.

3   Barth, "A Few Words," 6.

4   To Carver, the term "smacks of smallness of vision and execution"; "it's a
    label that bothers me," Carver says, "it suggests the idea of a narrow vision of
    life, low ambitions, and limited cultural horizons. And frankly, I don't believe
    that's my case." See Carver, Interview with Mona Simpson, 208, and Carver,
    "I'm Almost Their Father," Interview with Silvia Del Pozzo, 95. In minimalist
    art and music (in the symphonies of Phillip Glass or the sculptures of Robert
    Morris or David Smith, for instance), art objects tend to refer to themselves,
    mainly, with reminders coming in the form of repetitious notes or chords,
    on one hand, and in deliberately unfinished or underfinished surfaces, on the
    other. Realism and self-referentiality are hardly compatible terms. In the
    literary realm we see instances of "minimalism" in the later — and
    stranger — work of Gertrude Stein ("Tender Buttons," "Making of Ameri-
    cans") and the poetry of the Language Poets (Charles Bernstein, Susan Howe,
    Michael Palmer), in verbal artifacts concerned expressly with their own
    "objecthood."

5   Houston, "Inarticulateness," 23. For a fascinating, more technical investiga-
    tion of Carver's style, see Chénetier, "Living."

6   LeClair, "Fiction Chronicle," 87.

7   Mars-Jones, "Words," 76.

8   Embedded in the story also is a topical matter which Carver refers to
    elsewhere as the "baleful influence" of his children on his early years as artist
    and breadwinner, refracted as it is in the words of the photographer, who,
    referring to his children and raising his hooks, says, "They're what gave me
    this." Recalling his first marriage and its attendant struggles, Carver says, "I'd
    take poison before I'd go through that time again . . . My kids were in full cry
    then . . . and they were eating me alive." See "Fires," in Fires, 22–26; Jenks,

"Together in Carver Country," 117. See also Carver's "Jerry and Molly and Sam" and "The Compartment" for fictive variations on a common theme.

9  All references to this collection are cited from the Random House/Vintage, 1982 edition.

10  "Vitamins," in *Cathedral*, 107.

11  "On Writing," in *Fires*, 17.

12  For the genesis of this story see Carver, Interview with Mona Simpson, 208. Of related interest is a poem, "His Bathrobe Pockets Stuffed With Notes," appearing first in 1986 and collected in *A New Path to the Waterfall*, 64–66. One stanza reads, "The woman in El Paso who wants to give us her furniture/But it's clear she is having a nervous breakdown/We're afraid to touch it/Then we take the bed, and a chair."

13  Newlove, Donald, *What We Talk About*, 77.

14  Mars-Jones, "Words," 76.

15  "Dummy," in *Furious Seasons*, 22.

16  Carver's personal — and not unrelated — concerns about the disintegration and death of his own father appear in an essay, "My Father's Life."

17  *Furious Seasons*, 9.

18  *Furious Seasons*, 26.

19  "Gazebo," in "What We Talk About," 27.

20  Aristotle, *Poetics*, 103.

21  *Will You Please Be Quiet, Please?*

22  *Cathedral*.

23  Chénetier, "Living," 174, 180.

24  Longinus, in *Critical Theory Since Plato*, 94.

25  Wellek, *Theory of Literature*, 157.

26  Especially pertinent here are Carver's comments regarding his tendency to write short stories and poems rather than novels: "To write a novel," he explains, "a writer should be living in a world that makes sense, a world that the writer can believe in, draw a bead on, and then write about accurately. A world that will, for a time anyway, stay fixed in one place. Along with this there has to be a belief in the essential correctness of that world . . . This wasn't the case with the world I knew and was living in. My world was one that seemed to change gears, along with its rules, every day." See "Fires," in *Fires*, 26.

27  "On Writing," in *Fires*, 14.
28  Brooks, "The Language of Paradox," 298.
29  LeClair, "Fiction Chronicle," 87.
30  Carver, Interview with Mona Simpson, 210.
31  Carver, Interview with Hansmaarten Tromp, 16.
32  Gorra, "Laughter," 156; Bell, "Less," 67.
33  Carver, "On Writing," in *Fires*, 16.
34  Carver, Interview with David Sexton, 38.
35  Interview with Larry McCaffery, 78.
36  Interview with John Alton, 9.
37  Richard, "La quotidienneté américaine," 9.
38  Carver (citing Flaubert), Interview with Sylvia Del Pozzo, 95.
39  Phillips, "Secret Places," 77.

CHAPTER THREE

1  "The Compartment," in *Cathedral*, 48.
2  See "Collectors" and "Are You A Doctor?" in *Will You Please Be Quiet, Please?*
and "Gazebo" in *What We Talk About*.
3  "[M]en do get hit hard in many of the stories," Carver explains, in part
because they have responsible positions and "can't meet their responsibilities"; the women in his fiction, therefore, are "more apt to survive." See
Carver, Interview with John Alton, 9.
4  Skenazy, "Life in Limbo," 78.
5  Howe, "Stories," 1 ; Carver, Interview with Kay Bonetti, 21.
6  Howe, "Stories," 42.
7  Goodheart, "The Fiction of Raymond Carver," 25.
8  Carver, Interview with John Alton, 10.
9  For a brilliant narratological/stylistic analysis of this story see Verley, "Narration and Interiority."
10  Skenazy, "Life in Limbo," 83.
11  Saltzman, *Understanding Raymond Carver*, 147.
12  See also Carver's later story, "Elephant" (in *Where I'm Calling From*), in which
a reformed alcoholic refers to his drinking days, and his vision of alcoholic
relapse, as "rock bottom."

13  Stull, "Beyond Hopelessville," 11.

14  Describing the trajectory of Carver's fiction in figurative terms, Adam Meyer sees an "hourglass, beginning wide, then narrowing, and then widening out again" — an apt observation. See "Now You See Him," 239.

15  Shute, "Finding the Words," 6.

16  Stull, "Beyond Hopelessville," 11.

17  Stull, "Beyond Hopelessville," 9.

18  Gearheart, "Breaking the Ties that Bind," 444.

19  Carver, Interview with Larry McCaffery, in Gentry and Stull, *Conversations with Raymond Carver*, 102.

20  Shute, 6.

21  Stull, "Beyond Hopelessville," 9–10.

22  Carver, Interview with David Sexton, 38.

23  Skenazy, "Life in Limbo," 82.

24  Vander Weele, "Language of Desire," 120.

25  Howe, "Stories," 43.

26  For this coinage I am indebted to Barbara C. Lonnquist and her essay "Narrative Displacement and Literary Faith."

27  Goodheart, "The Fiction of Raymond Carver," 25.

28  Saltzman, *Understanding Raymond Carver*, 154.

29  Skenazy, "Life in Limbo," 83.

30  This bit of information I gleaned in a conversation with Tess Gallagher, who refutes Carver's assertion in his preface to the first edition of *Where I'm Calling From*, which reads, "After a good night's sleep, I went to my desk and wrote the story 'Cathedral.' "

31  Carver, Interview with David Sexton, 38.

32  Goodheart, "The Fiction of Raymond Carver," 25; *Where I'm Calling From*, preface to the first edition, i.

33  Carver, Interview with Larry McCaffery, in *Conversations*, 100.

34  Carver, and Jenks, eds., Introduction to *American Short Story Masterpieces*, xiii.


CHAPTER FOUR

1  Gallagher, Introduction to *A New Path to the Waterfall*, xxiii-iv.

2  *Waterfall*, 35.

3   Wolff, "Had His Cake," 248.
4   Saltzman, *Understanding Raymond Carver*, 175.
5   "Menudo," in *Where I'm Calling From*, 334.
6   Robinson, "Marriage," 40.
7   Skenazy, "Peering Through the Keyhole," 9.
8   "Mother," in *Ultramarine*, 128.
9   *What We Talk About When We Talk About Love*, 154.
10   Howe, "Stories," 42.
11   Saltzman, *Understanding Raymond Carver*, 175.
12   "Miracle," in *Waterfall*, 28.
13   For an even darker variant of this see "The Offending Eel," a poem in which an "unhappy" prince strangles on "a dish of eels." (*Waterfall*, 79–82).
14   In Hispanic cultures, it is worth mentioning here, menudo is a New Year's dish and is valued as such for its special spiritual and restorative properties.
15   "Fat," in *Will You Please Be Quiet, Please?*, 5.
16   "Yes," Tess Gallagher informs me (annotating an early draft of this chapter). "As we worked on this ending this is what we aimed for."
17   "Blackbird Pie," like "Boxes," has its genesis in a poem; for a rather different perspective on the problems of the story see "Late Night With Fog and Horses," in *Where Water Comes Together*, 100.
18   The genesis of this story lies in a poem, "The Mail," in *Ultramarine*, 13.
19   Robinson, "Marriage," 40.
20   Of related interest is Carver's "Drinking While Driving," in *Fires*, 14, and "I Know a Man" by Robert Creely — a poet Carver both read and admired.
21   Wolff, "Had His Cake," 248.
22   As one critic notes, it's always a kind of "uneasy laughter" that arises in the reading of a Carver story — a kind of humor which, as Carver describes it himself, is "close to pain." Discussing the comic aspects of "Where Is Everyone?" Carver explains that his humor "has a double edge to it. We laugh at it because if we didn't laugh at it . . . we could bawl our eyes out." Curiously, Carver was not immune to the humor of his stories; "The great thing about Ray," his friend Richard Ford says, "was that he loved to laugh. He just couldn't help himself. Sometimes in his readings he'd come to just about the blackest part of the story and he'd burst out laughing." See Carver, Interview with David Sexton, 40, and Seabrook, "Of Bird Dogs," 130.

23  *Will You Please Be Quiet, Please?*, 129; *What We Talk About*, 3; "Menudo," *Where I'm Calling From*, 338.

24  Robinson, "Marriage," 40.

25  *Waterfall*, 115, 111.

26  "If I'm lucky," Carver writes in a poem, "I'll be wired every which way/in a hospital bed. Tubes running into/my nose. But try not to be scared of me, friends!/ I'm telling you right now that this is okay. / It's little enough to ask for at the end." See "My Death," in *Where Water Comes Together*, 106–7.

27  See Stewart Kellerman, "Grace Has Come Into My Life," 40.

28  "Winter Insomnia," in *Winter Insomnia*, 23.

29  Carver, "On Writing," in *Fires*, 14.

30  Gallagher, Introduction to *Waterfall*, xxii.

31  Carver had been reading a translation of Henri Troyat's biography *Chekov* prior to the writing of "Errand"; Carver's account follows Troyat's quite closely and, in places, cites it. It is interesting to note the details Carver left out — for instance, that Chekov's friend's "were flabbergasted to learn that his coffin had traveled in a dirty green van with the word FOR OYSTERS written in large letters on the door" (*Chekov*, 333): such details put a curious spin on Carver's version of the story.

32  Gallagher, Introduction to *Waterfall*, xvii, xxvi. "[A]s we read the biography in part aloud," Tess has told me privately, "Ray seemed very baffled that Chekov, a doctor, could accept his own clear symptoms for so long."

33  A word-for-word citation from Troyat's biography.

34  Gallagher, Introduction to *Waterfall*, xxv.

35  Carver, Annotative remark on "Errand" in *Best American Short Stories* 1988, 319.

36  "The Meadow," in *Ultramarine*, 103.

37  *Fires*, 13–19.

38  "Where They'd Lived," in *Ultramarine*, 17. See also "Interview," in *Where Water Comes Together*, 79, and "The Author of Her Misfortune," in *Ultramarine*, 51.

39  Stafford, "Suddenly Everything Became Clear," 104.

40  Clark, "Final Chapter," 3.

41  Lepape, "Carver et Vautrin," 12 (my translation).

42  Carver, Interview with John Alton, 14.

43  Clute, "Reports," 532.

44  Carver, Interview with Kasia Boddy, 16.

45  Carver (citing Frank O'Connor), Interview with Larry McCaffery, in McCaffery, *Alive and Writing*, 78.

46  *London Times*, cited by Gallagher, Introduction to *Waterfall*, xxix. London's *Guardian* similarly called Carver "America's Chekov" in its obituary.

47  Goodheart, "The Fiction of Raymond Carver," 25.

48  Carver, Interview with Kay Bonetti, 23.

49  Carver, Interview with Mona Simpson, 221.

50  Carver, Interview with Mona Simpson, 221.

51  Carver, Introduction to *Best American Short Stories* 1986, xiv.

# Bibliography

Abrams, Linsey. "A Maximalist Novelist Looks at Some Minimalist Fiction."
Mississippi Review 40/41 (Winter 1985): 24–30.

Aristotle. Poetics. Literary Criticism Plato to Dryden. Ed. Allan H. Gilbert. Detroit:
Wayne State University Press, 1982. 69–124.

Atlas, James. "Less is Less." Atlantic 247.6 (June 1981): 96–98.

Auerbach, Erich. Mimesis. Princeton, NJ: Princeton University Press, 1953.

Bakhtin, M.M. The Dialogic Imagination. Trans. Caryl Emerson and Michael
Holquist. Austin: University of Texas Press, 1981.

Banks, Russell. "Raymond Carver: Our Stephen Crane." Atlantic 268.2 (August
1991): 99–103.

Barth, John. "Muse, Spare Me." Book Week, September 26, 1965: 28–29.

———. "The Literature of Exhaustion." Atlantic Monthly August 1967: 65–71.

———. "The Literature of Replenishment." Atlantic Monthly January 1980:
65–71.

———. " A Few Words About Minimalism." New York Times Book Review, December
28, 1986: Rpt. in Weber Studies 4.2 (Fall 1987): 5–14.

Barthelme, Frederick. "On Being Wrong: Convicted Minimalist Spills Bean."
New York Times Book Review, April 3, 1988.

Barthes, Roland. S/Z. Trans. Richard Miller. New York: Hill and Wang, 1974.

Bataille, Georges. Erotism. Trans. Mary Dalwood. San Francisco: City Lights, 1986.

Bate, Walter Jackson, ed. Criticism: The Major Texts. New York: Harcourt, Brace,
and World, 1952.

Beattie, Ann. "Carver's Furious Seasons." Canto 2.2 (Summer 1978): 178–82.

Begley, Adam. "Less and More." London Review of Books 10.16 (September 15,
1988): 17–18.

Bellamy, Joe David. *Harper's Bookletter*, April 26, 1976.

Bell, Madison. "Less is Less: The Dwindling American Short Story." *Harper's* 272.1631 (April 1986): 64–69.

Biguenet, John. "Notes of a Disaffected Reader: The Origins of Minimalism." *Mississippi Review* 40/41 (Winter 1985): 40–45.

Bloom, Harold. *The Visionary Company*. Ithaca: Cornell University Press, 1971.

Boddy, Kasia. "A Conversation." *London Review of Books*, September 15, 1988: 16.

Boxer, David, and Cassandra Phillips. "Will You Please Be Quiet, Please?: Voyeurism, Dissociation, and the Art of Raymond Carver." *Iowa Review* 10.3 (Summer 1979): 75–90.

Brooks, Cleanth. "The Language of Paradox." *Twentieth Century Literary Criticism*. Ed. David Lodge. New York: Longman, 1985. 292–304.

Brooks, Peter. *Reading For the Plot*. New York: Vintage/Random House, 1984.

Brown, Arthur A. "Raymond Carver and Postmodern Humanism." *Critique* 31.2 (Winter 1990): 125–36.

Brown, Norman O. *Life against Death: The Psychoanalytical Meaning of History*. New York: Vintage, 1959.

Buford, Bill. "Everything Going Wrong." T L S 4220 (February 17, 1984): 159.

Bugeja, Michael J. "Tarnish and Silver: An Analysis of Carver's *Cathedral*." *South Dakota Review* 24.3 (Autumn 1986): 73–87.

Burke, Kenneth. *Language as Symbolic Action*. Berkeley: University of California Press, 1966.

Buzbee, Lewis. "New Hope For the Dead — Raymond Carver 1939–1988" [sic]. *San Francisco Review of Books* 13.3 (Winter 1988–89): 31–32.

Campbell, Ewing. "Raymond Carver and the Literature of Subtraction." *Balcones Review* 1.1 (Spring 1987): 69–71.

———. "Raymond Carver's Therapeutics of Passion." *Journal of the Short Story in English* 16 (Spring 1991): 9–18.

———. *Raymond Carver: A Study of the Short Fiction*. Twayne's Studies in Short Fiction Series 31. New York: Twayne, 1992.

Campbell, Joseph. *The Hero with a Thousand Faces*. Cleveland: Meridian, 1956.

Carpenter, David. "What We Talk About When We Talk About Carver." *Descant* [Toronto] 56/57 (Spring-Summer 1987): 20–43.

Carver, Raymond. *Near Klamath*. Sacramento: English Club of Sacramento State College, 1968.

———. *Winter Insomnia*. Santa Cruz: Kayak, 1970.

———. *Put Yourself in My Shoes*. Santa Barbara: Capra, 1974.

———. *At Night the Salmon Move*. Santa Barbara: Capra, 1976.

———. *Will You Please Be Quiet, Please?* New York: McGraw-Hill, 1976.

———. *Furious Seasons and Other Stories*. Santa Barbara: Capra, 1977.

———. *What We Talk About When We Talk About Love*. New York: Knopf, 1981. Rpt. *What We Talk About When We Talk About Love*. New York: Random House/ Vintage, 1982.

———. *Cathedral*. New York: Knopf, 1983.

———. *Fires: Essays, Poems, Stories*. Santa Barbara: Capra, 1983.

———. Interview with Mona Simpson. "The Art of Fiction LXXVI." *Paris Review* 25.88 (Summer 1983): 192–221.

———. Interview with Kay Bonetti. *Saturday Review* September-October 1983: 21–23.

———. *If It Please You*. Northridge, CA: Lord John, 1984.

———. Interview with Hansmaarten Tromp. Trans. Stephan T. Moskey. *Haagse Post* [Amsterdam], August 4, 1984: 1–18.

———. *Where Water Comes Together with Other Water*. New York: Random, 1985.

———, and Tess Gallagher. *Dostoevsky: A Screenplay*. Santa Barbara: Capra, 1985.

———. Interview with David Sexton. *Literary Review* [London] 85 (July 1985): 36–40.

———. "My Father's Life." Derry, NH: Babcock & Koontz, 1986. Rpt. in *Fires* Random House/Vintage, 1989.

———. *Ultramarine*. New York: Random, 1986.

———. Interview with Sylvia Del Pozzo. Trans. Susanna Peters Coy. *Panorama*. March 23, 1986: 95.

———. *In a Marine Light: Selected Poems*. London: Collins Harvill, 1987.

———. *Those Days: Early Writings by Raymond Carver*. Ed. William L. Stull. Elmwood: Raven, 1987.

———. Interview with Larry McCaffery. *Alive and Writing*. Ed. Sinda Gregory and Larry McCaffery. Chicago: University of Illinois Press, 1987: 66–82.

———. Contribution to "A Symposium of Contemporary American Fiction." *Michigan Quarterly Review* 26 (Fall 1987): 710–11.

———. *Elephant and Other Stories*. London: Collins Harvill, 1988.

———. *Where I'm Calling From: New and Selected Stories*. New York: Atlantic Monthly, 1988.

——. Annotative remark on "Errand." *Best American Short Stories 1988.* Ed. Mark Helprin. Boston: Houghton-Mifflin, 1988. 319.

——. Interview with Michael Schumacher. *Reasons to Believe.* Ed. Michael Schumacher. New York: Saint Martin's, 1988. 1–27.

——. Interview with John Alton. *Chicago Review* 36.2 (Autumn 1988): 4–21.

——. Interview with Kasia Boddy. *London Review of Books,* September 15, 1988: 16.

——. Interview with William Stull, "Matters of Life and Death," in *Living in Words,* ed. Gregory McNamee, (Portland: Breitenbush, 1988).

——. *A New Path to the Waterfall.* New York: Atlantic Monthly, 1989.

——. *Carver Country: The World of Raymond Carver.* With photographs by Bob Adelman. New York: Scribner's, 1990.

——. *Conversations with Raymond Carver.* Ed. Marshall Bruce Gentry and William L. Stull. Jackson: University Press of Mississippi, 1990.

——. *No Heroics, Please: Uncollected Writings.* Ed. William L. Stull. London: Collins Harvill, 1991; New York: Vintage, 1992.

——. *Carnations.* Ed. William L. Stull. Vineburg: Engdahl Typography, 1992.

Carver, Raymond and Tom Jenks, eds., *American Short Story Masterpieces.* New York: Delacorte, 1987.

Carver, Raymond with Shannon Ravenel. *The Best American Short Stories 1986.* Boston: Houghton, 1986.

Cheever, John. *The Stories of John Cheever.* New York: Alfred A. Knopf, 1979.

Chénetier, Marc. *Au-delà du soupçon: La nouvelle fiction américaine de 1960 à nos jours.* Paris: Seuil, 1989.

——. "Living On/Off the 'Reserve': Performance, Interrogation, and Negativity in the Works of Raymond Carver." *Critical Angles: European Views of Contemporary American Literature.* Ed. Chénetier, Marc. Carbondale: Southern Illinois University Press, 1986. 164–90.

Clark, Tom. "Raymond Carver's Final Chapter." *San Francisco Times Book Review,* July 2, 1989: 3.

Clarke, Graham. "Investing the Glimpse: Raymond Carver and the Syntax of Silence." *The New American Writing: Essays on American Literature Since 1970.* New York: St. Martin's Press, 1990. 99–122.

Clute, John. "Word-Danger." *Times Literary Supplement* 4286 (May 24, 1985): 572.

——. "Reports from the Regions." *Times Literary Supplement* 4441 (May 13, 1988): 532.

Coover, Robert. Interview with David Applefield. "Fiction and America." *Frank* [Paris] 8/9 (Winter 1987–88): 6–15.

Cushman, Keith. "Blind, Intertextual Love: 'The Blind Man' and Raymond Carver's 'Cathedral.'" *Etudes Lawrenciennes* 3 (1988): 125–38.

Daiches, David. *The Novel and the Modern World.* Chicago: University of Chicago Press, 1939.

Dana, Robert. "In the Labyrinth: Poetry as Prose; Prose as Poetry." *North American Review* 275.3 (September 1990): 72–80.

Dardis, Tom. *The Thirsty Muse: Alcohol and the American Writer.* New York: Ticknor & Fields, 1989.

Day, R. C. "Raymond Carver: A Remembrance." *Toyon* 35 (Spring 1989): 20.

Delbanco, Nicholas, ed. "A Symposium on Contemporary American Fiction." *Michigan Quarterly Review,* 26.4 (Fall 1987): 679–802; 27.1 (Winter 1988): 79–135. Rpt. in *Writers and Their Craft: Short Stories and Essays on the Narrative.* Eds. Nicholas Delbanco and Laurence Goldstein. Detroit: Wayne State University Press, 1991. 47–235.

de Man, Paul. *Blindness and Insight: Essays in the Rhetoric of Contemporary Fiction.* New York: Oxford University Press, 1971.

DeMarinis, Rick. *Under the Wheat.* Pittsburgh: University of Pittsburgh Press, 1986.

Dempsey, David. "Up, Up and Away with the Short Story." *Antioch Review* 42.2 (Spring 1984): 247–55.

Derrida, Jacques. *Positions.* Trans. Alan Bass. Chicago: University of Chicago Press, 1981.

Duranti, Riccardo. "Ricordo di Raymond Carver." *Linea d'ombra* 32 (November 1988): 87–88.

Eagleton, Terry. *Literary Theory.* Minneapolis: University of Minnesota Press, 1983.

Eichman, Erich. "Will Raymond Carver Please Be Quiet, Please?" *New Criterion* 2.3 (November 1983): 86–89.

Eliade, Mircea. *Myth and Reality.* New York: Harper, 1968.

Ellison, Ralph. "Society, Morality, and the Novel." *The Living Novel: A Symposium.* Ed. Granville Hicks. New York: Macmillan, 1957.

Federman, Raymond, ed. *Surfiction: Fiction Now and Tomorrow.* Chicago: Swallow Press, 1975.

Fiedler, Leslie. *Love and Death in the American Novel.* New York: Criterion Books, 1960.

Fisketjon, Gary L. "Normal Nightmares." The Village Voice, September 18, 1978, 132ff.

Flower, Dean. "Fiction Chronicle." Hudson Review 29.2 (Summer 1976): 270–82.

Fontana, Ernest. "Insomnia in Raymond Carver's Fiction." Studies in Short Fiction 26.4 (Fall 1989): 447–51.

Frank, Joseph. The Widening Gyre: Crisis and Mastery in Modern Literature. Bloomington: Indiana University Press, 1968.

Gallagher, Tess. "Raymond Carver, 1938 to 1988." Granta 25 (Autumn 1988): 163–67.

———. Introduction. A New Path to the Waterfall. By Raymond Carver. New York: Atlantic Monthly Press, 1989. xxii-xxxi.

———. "Carver Country." Carver, Carver Country, 8–19.

Gardner, John. On Moral Fiction. New York: Basic Books, 1978.

Gass, William H. Fiction and the Figures of Life. New York: Alfred A. Knopf, 1970.

Gearhart, Michael William. "Breaking the Ties That Bind: Inarticulation in the Fiction of Raymond Carver." Studies in Short Fiction 26.4 (Fall 1989): 439–46.

German, Norman, and Jack Bedell. "Physical and Social Laws in Ray Carver's 'Popular Mechanics.'" Critique 29.4 (Summer 1988): 257–60.

Gilder, Joshua. "Less Is Less." New Criterion 1.6 (February 1983): 78–82.

Goodheart, Eugene. "The Fiction of Raymond Carver." Boston Review 9.1 (February 1984): 25.

Gorra, Michael. "Laughter and Bloodshed." Hudson Review 37.1 (Spring 1984): 151–64.

Graff, Gerald. Literature against Itself: Literary Ideas in Modern Society. Chicago: University of Chicago Press, 1979.

Grimal, Claude. "La limpidité mystérieuse de Raymond Carver." La quinzaine littéraire 526 (February 16, 1989): 8–9.

———. "L'écrivain à l'oeuvre." La quinzaine littéraire 576 (April 16, 1991): 5.

Halpert, Sam, ed. When We Talk About Raymond Carver. Layton: Peregrine Smith, 1991.

Haslam, Thomas J. " 'Where I'm Calling From': A Textual and Critical Study." Studies in Short Fiction 29.1 (Winter 1992): 57–65.

Hathcock, Nelson. " 'The Possibility of Resurrection': Re-Vision in Carver's 'Feathers' and 'Cathedral.' " Studies in Short Fiction 28.1 (Winter 1991): 31–39.

Henning, Barbara. "Minimalism and the American Dream: 'Shiloh' by Bobbie

Ann Mason and 'Preservation' by Raymond Carver." *Modern Fiction Studies* 35.4 (Winter 1989): 689–98.

Herzinger, Kim A. "Introduction: On the New Fiction." *Mississippi Review* 40/41 (Winter 1985): 7–22.

Houston, Robert. "A Stunning Inarticulateness." *Nation* 233.1 (July 4, 1981): 23–25.

Howe, Irving. "Stories of Our Loneliness." *New York Times Book Review*, September 11, 1983.

Iser, Wolfgang. *The Implied Reader: Patterns of Communication in Prose Fiction from Bunyan to Beckett.* Baltimore: Johns Hopkins University Press, 1974.

Jakobson, Roman, and M. Halle. *Fundamentals of Language.* The Hague: Mouton, 1956.

Jenks, Tom. "Together in Carver Country." *Vanity Fair* 49.10 (October 1986): 114ff.

Karlsson, Ann-Marie. "The Hyperrealistic Short Story: A Postmodern Twilight Zone." *Criticism in the Twilight Zone: Postmodern Perspectives on Literature and Politics.* Eds. Danuta Zadworna-Fjellestad and Lennart Björk. Stockholm Studies in English 77. Stockholm: Almqvist, 1990. 144–53.

Kaufmann, David. "Yuppie Postmodernism." *Arizona Quarterly* 47.2 (Summer 1991): 93–116.

Kellerman, Stewart. "Grace Has Come into My Life." *New York Times Book Review*, May 15, 1988: 40.

Kermode, Frank. *The Sense of an Ending: Studies in the Theory of Fiction.* New York: Oxford University Press, 1968.

Kittredge, William. *We Are Not In This Together.* Port Townsend, WA: Graywolf Press, 1984.

———. "from Hole in the Sky." *Ploughshares* 16.4 (Winter 1990–91): 224–54.

Klinkowitz, Jerome. *Literary Disruptions: The Making of a Post-Contemporary American Fiction.* Urbana: University of Illinois Press, 1975.

———. "The Effacement of Contemporary American Literature." *College English* 42.4 (1980): 382–89.

Kubal, David. "Fiction Chronicle." *Hudson Review* 34.3 (Autumn 1981): 456–66.

Kuzma, Greg. "Ultramarine: Poems That Almost Stop the Heart." *Michigan Quarterly Review* 27.2 (Spring 1988): 355–63.

Lacan, Jacques. *The Language of the Self.* Trans. and ed. Anthony Wilden. New York: Delta, 1975.

Laing, R.D. *The Divided Self*. Baltimore: Penguin, 1965.

LeClair, Thomas. "Fiction Chronicle — June 1981." *Contemporary Literature* 23.1 (Winter 1982): 83–91.

Lentricchia, Frank. *After the New Criticism*. Chicago: University of Chicago Press, 1980.

Lepape, Pierre. "Carver et Vautrin: une même compassion." *Le Monde* 2100 (January 26, 1989): 12.

Lohafer, Susan. *Coming to Terms with the Short Story*. Baton Rouge: Louisiana State University Press, 1983.

Longinus. *Critical Theory Since Plato*. Ed. Hazard Adams. New York: Harcourt Brace, 1971. 77–102.

Lonnquist, Barbara C. "Narrative Displacement and Literary Faith: Raymond Carver's Inheritance from Flannery O'Connor." *Since Flannery O'Connor: Essays on the Contemporary American Short Story*. Eds. Loren Logsdon and Charles W. Mayer. An *Essays in Literature* Book. Macomb: Western Illinois University Press, 1987. 142–50.

Malamet, Elliott. "Raymond Carver and the Fear of Narration." *Journal of the Short Story in English* 17 (Autumn 1991): 59–74.

Mars-Jones, Adam. "Words for the Walking Wounded." *Times Literary Supplement* 4112 (January 22, 1982): 76.

McCaffery, Larry, ed. *Postmodern Fiction: A Bio-Bibliographical Guide*. Movements in the Arts Series 2. Westport: Greenwood, 1986.

McConnell, Frank D. *Four Postwar American Novelists*. Chicago: University of Chicago Press, 1977.

McInerney, Jay. "Raymond Carver: A Still, Small Voice." *New York Times Book Review* August 6, 1989.

McLuhan, Marshall. *The Gutenberg Galaxy: The Making of Typographic Man*. New York: Signet, 1969.

Meyer, Adam. "Now You See Him, Now You Don't, Now You Do Again: The Evolution of Raymond Carver's Minimalism." *Critique* 30.4 (Summer 1989): 239–51. Rpt. in Campbell, *Raymond Carver*, 143–58.

Miller, J. Hillis. "Poets of Reality." *The Secret Agent: A Casebook*. Ed. Ian Watt. London: Macmillan, 1973.

Mitchell, W.J.T., ed. *On Narrative*. Chicago: University of Chicago Press, 1981.

Nesset, Kirk. " 'This Word Love': Sexual Politics and Silence in Early Raymond Carver." *American Literature* 63.2 (June 1991): 293–313.

——. "The Final Stitch: Raymond Carver and Metaphor." *Profils Americains* 4 (Spring 1993): 21–27.

Newlove, Donald. "What We Talk About When We Talk About Love." *Saturday Review* April 1981: 77.

Olderman, Raymond M. *Beyond the Waste Land: A Study of the American Novel in the Nineteen-Sixties*. New Haven: Yale University Press, 1972.

Phillips, Jayne Anne. "The Secret Places of the Heart." *New York* 14.16 (April 20, 1981): 77–78.

Plath, James. "When Push Comes to Pull: Raymond Carver and the 'Popular Mechanics' of Divorce." *Notes on Contemporary Literature* 20.3 (May 1990): 2–4.

Pope, Dan. "The Post-Minimalist American Short Story or What Comes After Carver?" *The Gettysburg Review* 1.2 (Spring 1988): 331–42.

Richard, Claude. "La quotidienneté américaine." Trans. William Stull. *Quinzaine Litteraire* 439 (May 1–15, 1985): 8–9.

Richards, I. A. *Practical Criticism*. New York: Harcourt, Brace, and World, 1929.

Robinson, Marilynne. "Marriage and Other Astonishing Bonds." *New York Times Book Review*, May 15, 1988.

Robison, James C. "1969–1980: Experiment and Tradition." *The American Short Story 1945–1980: A Critical History*. Ed. Gordon Weaver. Boston: Twayne, 1983.

Saltzman, Arthur M. *Understanding Raymond Carver*. Columbia: University of South Carolina Press, 1988.

Sanders, Scott Russell. "Speaking a Word for Nature." *Michigan Quarterly Review* 26.4 (Fall 1987): 648–62. Rpt. in Delbanco, *Writers and Their Craft*, 394–407.

Scholes, Robert. *The Fabulators*. New York: Oxford University Press, 1967.

Seabrook, John. Interview with Richard Ford. "Of Bird Dogs and Tall Tales." *Interview* XIX.5 (May 1985): 128ff.

Shute, Kathleen Westfall. "Finding the Words: The Struggle for Salvation in the Fiction of Raymond Carver." *Hollins Critic* 24.5 (December 1987): 1–9. Rpt. in Campbell, *Raymond Carver*, 119–30.

Skenazy, Paul. "Peering through the Keyhole at Gloom." *Los Angeles Times Book Review*, June 26, 1988.

——. "Life in Limbo: Raymond Carver's Fiction." *Enclitic* 11.1 (21) (Fall 1988): 77–83.

Smith, Allan Lloyd. "Brain Damage: The Word and the World in Postmodernist

Writing." *Contemporary American Fiction.* Eds. Malcolm Bradbury and Sigmund Ro. Stratford-upon-Avon Studies, 2nd series. London: Edward Arnold, 1987. 39–50.

Smitten, Jeffrey, and Ann Daghistany, eds. *Spatial Form in Narrative.* Ithaca: Cornell University Press, 1981.

Solotaroff, Ted. "Raymond Carver: Going Through the Pain." *American Poetry Review* 18.2 (March-April 1989): 47–49.

Stafford, William. "Suddenly Everything Became Clear to Him." *Washington* 5.3 (November 1988): 103–06.

Stone, Robert. Untitled introductory statement to Carver, "Intimacy," *Esquire* (August 1986), 58.

Stull, William L. "Visions and Revisions." *Chariton Review* 10.1 (Spring 1984): 80–86.

——. "Raymond Carver." *Dictionary of Literary Biography Yearbook 1984.* Ed. Jean W. Ross. Detroit: Gale, 1985. 233–45.

——. "Beyond Hopelessville: Another Side of Raymond Carver." *Philological Quarterly* 64.1 (Winter 1985): 1–15.

——. "Raymond Carver: A Bibliographical Checklist." *American Book Collector* ns 8.1 (January 1987): 17–30.

——. "Raymond Carver Remembered: Three Early Stories." *Studies in Short Fiction,* 25.4 (Fall 1988): 461–77.

——. "Raymond Carver." *Dictionary of Literary Biography Yearbook 1988.* Ed. J.M. Brook. Detroit: Gale, 1989. 199–213.

——. "Raymond Carver." *Encyclopedia of World Literature in the 20th Century.* Eds. Steven R. Serafin and Walter D. Glanze. 4 vols. New York: Continuum, 1993. 120–21. Supplement.

——, with Maureen P. Carroll. *Remembering Ray.* Santa Barbara: Capra, 1993.

Tanner, Tony. *City of Words: American Fiction, 1950–1970.* New York: Harper and Row, 1971.

Towers, Robert. "Low-Rent Tragedies." *New York Review of Books* 38.8 (May 14, 1981): 37–40.

Troyat, Henri. *Chekov.* Trans. Michael Heim. New York: Dutton, 1986.

Vander Weele, Michael. "Raymond Carver and the Language of Desire." *Denver Quarterly* 22.1 (Summer 1987): 108–22.

Verley, Claudine. " 'Errand,' ou le réalisme de R. Carver dans un bouchon de champagne." *La nouvelle de langue anglaise* 7 (1991): 43–61.

———. "Narration and Interiority in Raymond Carver's 'Where I'm Calling From.' " *Journal of the Short Story in English* 13 (Autumn 1989): 91–102.

———. "The Window and the Eye in Carver's 'Boxes.'" *Journal of the Short Story in English* 15 (Autumn 1990): 95–106.

Wellek and Warren. *Theory of Literature.* New York: Harcourt Brace, 1956.

Wolff, Tobias. "Raymond Carver Had His Cake and Ate It Too." *Esquire* 112.3 (September 1989): 240ff.

Wood, Michael. "Stories Full of Edges and Silences." *New York Times Book Review,* April 26, 1981.

Yardley, Jonathan. "Raymond Carver's American Dreamers." *Washington Post Book World,* May 15, 1988: 3.

Young, Philip. *Three Bags Full: Essays in American Fiction.* New York: Harcourt Brace Jovanovich, 1972.

# Index

## A Note about the Author

Kirk Nesset is a novelist, short story writer, poet, essayist, and Assistant Professor of English and Writer-in-Residence at Whittier College. He is the father of an eleven-year-old daughter, Vanessa.

## About the Type

This book is set in Joanna, a typeface designed by Eric Gill in 1930 and produced by Monotype in 1937 for machine composition. Gill lived during the years 1882–1940. He earned a reputation as a renowned stone carver, illustrator, writer, and designer. Gill is also credited with the creation of the typefaces Gill Sans and Perpetua. The typeface Joanna was named in honor of Gill's daughter, Joan. The italic version has a slope of only three degrees and was made available in 1931.